A World *of* Noodles

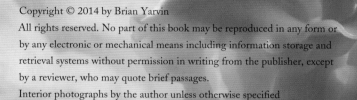

Book design and composition by Karen Schober Design
Published by The Countryman Press, P.O. Box 748,
Woodstock, VT 05091
Distributed by W. W. Norton & Company, Inc., 500 Fifth Avenue,
New York, NY 10110
Printed in the United States of America

10 9 8 7 6 5 4 3 2 1

Library of Congress Cataloging-in-Publication Data are available.
A World of Noodles
978-1-58157-210-0

A WORLD *of* NOODLES

BRIAN YARVIN

COUNTRYMAN PRESS
WOODSTOCK, VERMONT

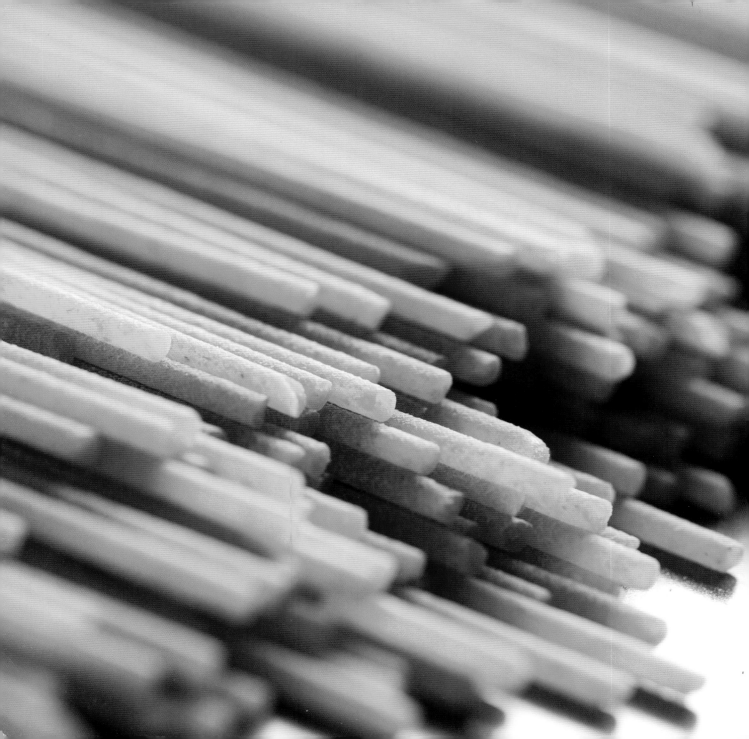

CONTENTS

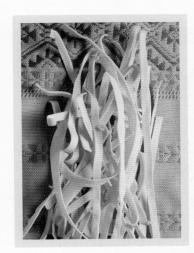

ITALY

Part III: A World of Noodles   128

KOREA

INTRODUCTION

In front of you is a bowl of soup with a nest of noodles, the broth nutty with soy sauce, the noodles thick and somehow almost fluffy. As a pat of butter melts into the mix, you inhale the steam and have a moment of enlightenment: this is Japan in an edible form. Or the dish may be elbows of macaroni comfortably couched in melted cheddar cheese. Maybe you're curious enough to wonder how they got those tiny pieces of pasta formed into little pipes, but more likely you're reveling in one of America's most pervasive comfort foods; yes, this is American culture in *its* edible form. It doesn't stop there. The plate in front of you could be a tangle of noodles painted with a kaleidoscope of spices, pork bits, and seafood—Thailand, of course. Make that sauce bright red with a touch of fragrant garlic, and Italy is right there and waiting for you.

All these dishes define their national cuisines, and all are noodles; little more than flour, water, and—maybe—some form of oil. In fact, more national cuisines are defined by noodles than any other ingredient. They're eaten on every continent, at every meal, and can be anything from street food to the most elegant haute cuisine.

JUST WHAT ARE NOODLES, ANYWAY?

Over the years, thousands of cookbooks have offered recipes for noodles, pasta, macaroni, and vermicelli, yet none seem to have bothered to tell you what they are, exactly. Yes, most will debunk the Marco Polo story about how noodles made their way from Asia to Europe, and many will detail noodle dishes from ancient Greece and Rome (as well as ancient China, of course), and others will tell of how Italian princesses brought noodle cuisine with them when they married into foreign royalty, but what noodles actually are? *The Art of Spaghetti Cookery,* by Myra Waldo (Doubleday, 1964), is typical. There's no real definition of the title ingredient. From page 1, readers are simply expected to know. Myra does introduce us to the word *pasta,* a term so common today that we forget that English-speaking nations have been using it in regular conversation for less than thirty years.

So here we are with a food that spans the globe, and numerous words that refer to it: *pasta, macaroni, vermicelli, spaghetti,* and, of course, *noodles.* We could use a definition. Here's mine: A food made from a dough of flour, water, and possibly oil and seasonings, and cooked using moist heat.

Pasta is the Italian word for dough; it came into English as a collective word for all those Italian noodle shapes and is now used as a synonym for *noodles.* I've heard people refer to "cold, Korean pasta soups" and "traditional Peruvian pasta dishes." In this book, we'll use the word *pasta* both interchangeably with *noodles* and in its Italian sense as a collective description of all those shapes. In times past, *vermicelli* and *macaroni* were also used as collective nouns for what we now call noodles or pasta. When you see those words in this book, they'll mean specific shapes and types, not general groups.

There's another aspect to the definition that isn't so scientific. Most of us think of noodles as long and thin or ribbonlike. The recipes in this book will reflect that. Sure, you'll see ways to cook ziti, orecchiette, and penne, but for the most part, we'll stick with the long stuff. That leaves us with a whole planet's worth of noodles.

DURUM, SEMOLINA, AND THE HISTORY OF WHEAT

The words *durum* and *semolina* show up on dry pasta boxes everywhere. What do they mean? A quick look at the history of wheat will give us the answer.

Thousands of years ago, there was only wild wheat, what we'd call emmer today. When agriculture began, the emmer seed was one of the first that people tried to cultivate. It was relatively easy to grow and had a property that other grains like millet and barley didn't share, the ability to be kneaded. You could make a porridge or flatbread out of any of them, but only emmer would develop the elasticity and texture we look for in bread, cakes, and, of course, noodles.

For those first farmers, it wasn't a big step from indiscriminately planting seeds to planting only the ones that had favored characteristics. From this point on, there were differences between wild and cultivated wheats. In some places, great effort is put into growing wheat that has the same properties of the wheat grown thousands of years ago, and Americans can often find noodles made with this flour under the name *farro* (also from the Italian).

As farming progressed, more and more different types of wheat became available, and the language of "hard" and "soft" evolved to describe them: soft (or, alternatively, weak), meaning less gluten, and hard, meaning more. (Note: If you're feeding people on gluten-free diets, avoid all wheat, no matter the stated gluten content. No exceptions!) It didn't stop there; extra-hard varieties of wheat became known by the Latin word for hard, *durum*. Flour from durum wheat is ideal for making dry pastas; doughs made with it do a better job of holding their shape during both drying and cooking.

But wait, there's more . . . so far, we've only discussed the grain itself. How it's ground matters too. Grind the whole grain of harvested wheat into a powder and you have whole wheat flour; remove the seed germ and it's white flour. Grind it a bit more coarsely and you have semolina, with individual grains that are too big for baking but perfect for pasta.

In modern flour production, the wheat grains are passed between progressively narrower rollers until the resulting product has the desired degree of fineness. You can say that wheat is first ground into semolina, and then semolina is ground into flour. Durum semolina is the coarse-ground flour from durum wheat.

Can you have whole grain durum semolina with the wheat germ still there? It's not common. If it's something you want, search hard and read your labels carefully.

THE FIRST NOODLES: A BIT OF ARCHAEOLOGY

Some recipes are considered old because they can be traced back to the 1920s. Noodles are older than that, though. Descriptions of noodles that are two thousand years old or more have been found in several parts of the world, but the current record goes to a bowl of actual noodles discovered in Lajia, on the Yellow River in China.

Lajia is a sort of Chinese Pompeii. Silt from a sudden flood preserved the site in a way that would be hard to do otherwise, giving us a snapshot of life four thousand years ago. Among the human remains and household items found by excavators was a bowl of noodles. A clay bowl of

actual noodles—not made of wheat or rice, but noodles still. Although described by researchers as resembling the hand-pulled noodles still found in parts of China today, analysis showed that the noodles were made from millet, a grain unlikely to have enough gluten to do the serious stretching that hand pulling requires. With-out access to the millet flour in use in the region thousands of years ago, there's no way to tell for sure, but I'll take an educated guess and say that these noodles were rolled out and cut into strips, a method that works with all sorts of grains. Millet dough may handle like a rice dough, but it's likely that it had a taste more like soba (see page 92). Deep, nutty, and a bit assertive, in the opinion of many modern eaters.

Chinese historians sometimes attribute the invention of hand-pulled noodles to the superior skills of imperial chefs, but a much more likely explanation would be the introduction of wheat. Reading between the lines, this could very well mean that while the Chinese were eating what we'd today call noodles long before anybody else, they didn't take their present form until wheat was introduced thousands of years later.

Does this mean that the different aspects of noodle making evolved in different places? Today, it doesn't seem like there's anything more to noodles than flour, water, and maybe an egg, but if you didn't have any one of those components, it would have been a big deal when you found one.

Imagine being the first person to knead wheat flour. Instead of the usual thick paste made from other grains, it suddenly became elastic. You could stretch it and pull it into long strings. Boil the dough and it had a chew to it that no other grain offered. Bake it and the combination of bread and crust was like nothing else ever tasted.

Noodles made their way across the world the same way so many other foods did: via the Silk Road—that long trade route that led from Europe to China. Those Silk Road traders who many of us imagine as ancient backpackers carried so much: not just spices, but chicken, lamb, wheat, and rice. And they didn't just dump those products at their customers' feet, they taught them how they were to be cultivated, cooked, and eaten.

Has the Silk Road trader Marco Polo become a symbolic stand-in for the thousands of people who wandered the trail carrying wonders to sell? Surely, the famous Venetian wasn't the first to carry pasta between China and Italy; both countries had been eating noodles for a very long time before his travels. But the trail is the real inventor, the road that brought together kneading, rolling, boiling, wheat, and seasonings, enabling us to sit down to a helping of noodles today.

THE BASICS

TOOLS OF THE TRADE

Noodles are among the most ancient of prepared foods and certainly predate the huge inventory of gadgets that some experts tell you you'll need. You can cook many—if not most—of the recipes in this book with a pot for boiling the noodles, a large skillet for making the sauces, a couple of wooden spoons for stirring, a good kitchen knife, a strainer (if you only get one, buy the kind with a handle so you can reserve the boiling water), and measuring cups and spoons to dole out the right amounts of ingredients.

Some of the recipes will ask you to make your own pasta dough. For this, you'll need a flat surface, a rolling pin, and perhaps a wooden rack for drying the noodles after they're formed. A hand-cranked pasta machine will make this task much easier, and some of the recipes in this book call for one. Please promise me, though, that you'll only buy a pasta machine if you intend to use it fairly often. Of course, if you're a noodle fan, you should both own one and use it. Remember that the expense of buying the machine will be offset by the low cost of homemade noodles; a couple of batches a month would easily make up for the initial outlay.

Anything else? A baking dish for things like ziti (page 52) and kugel (page 239), a stock pot or Dutch oven for dishes like chicken noodle soup, a cutting board to work on, some kitchen tongs to grasp hot items in the pot, and some pot holders to grab the pots themselves. Don't overdo it! The more stuff you use, the more stuff you have to clean afterward. Instead, use the money you save to buy something delicious—you have my permission.

FRESH NOODLES

People have been making noodles for thousands of years; they've even been found in ancient Chinese tombs. I'm not surprised by this at all; once they're dry, noodles can last almost forever, waiting patiently until you bring them to life in a pot of boiling water and define yourself culturally by choosing a sauce.

While almost everything has been added to the mix at one time or another, there are three basic ingredients: flour, water, and salt. That's it. Except that it isn't. The flour you choose is important. Most of us think of flour as the bag of white stuff that starts leaking even before you get it home from the supermarket. There's more, though—it comes in thousands of varieties: on store shelves, you'll see all-purpose, bread, cake, and others too. When it comes to noodle making, you can safely ignore bleached white flour and cake flour. Both are important in baking, but make a dough that's too mushy for noodles, something you almost certainly wind up eating with a fork or chopsticks. The ideal flour is durum semolina.

Durum semolina sounds like it should be rare and difficult to find. Yet, because it's the basic building block of dried pasta, it's grown all over the place and sold in markets that cater to serious cooks. What is it? Durum wheat is a variety that's very high in protein and low in gluten. This means it's easier to roll into the right shapes. It also gives that famous al dente texture that people talk about (*al dente* is Italian for "at teeth"; that is, you can feel the firmness of the cooked noodles at your teeth when you chew them). Semolina is the way the flour is ground. Indeed, a handful of semolina is coarser and yellower than an equal amount of all-purpose. So flour can be semolina but not durum and durum but not semolina. Your ideal noodle flour is both.

Basic Noodles

The basic formula for fresh noodles is easy: for every cup of flour add half a cup of water, and then follow the instructions for mixing and kneading.

1. Combine the water and flour in a large bowl. Mix until a dough forms, first with a wooden spoon, and then with your hands. If the mixture is too liquid, add flour, 1 tablespoon at a time, until it can be formed into a kneadable ball. If the mixture is too dry, add water, 1 tablespoon at a time, until the dough is soft enough to knead.

2. Sprinkle some flour on a flat surface and knead the dough. After about 5 minutes, it will be springy and elastic with gluten; this is the bread stage. For great noodles, you need to go beyond the bread stage and knead until the dough holds the shape you form it into without springing back, about 10 minutes.

3. Wrap the dough in a kitchen towel or plastic wrap and let it rest for at least 30 minutes before rolling it out. This gives the flour grains a chance to fully absorb the water. If you're making the dough ahead of time, refrigerate or freeze it after you knead it and before you roll it out.

ROLLING THE DOUGH While the dough can be flattened and shaped with a rolling pin—or even pounded with a flat stone— nothing is better suited to the task than a pasta machine (see

MAKES 4 SERVINGS

2 cups flour* + flour for kneading and drying

1 cup water

*While it must be wheat flour, you can use unbleached all-purpose, durum semolina, or a mixture of half all-purpose and half whole wheat.

"Tools of the Trade," page 19). Once you have your machine firmly attached to your table (it comes with a clamp for this purpose), start by pressing a small amount of dough into a pancake between your palms. Then on the machine's thickest setting—almost always marked "1"— start cranking the dough through. After four or five trips through the pasta machine, the dough should stay flat and smooth and hold its shape. Then change the thickness to setting 2 and repeat. Keep rolling it through thinner and thinner settings until you have what you need—4 will suffice for a simple linguine or tagliatelle; 5 or 6 for angel hair or other fine shapes.

CUTTING AND DRYING THE NOODLES Your pasta machine will also have a setting for cutting the pasta sheets into strands. Once your strands are cut, lay them out on a drying rack or sheet of floured parchment paper to dry. If you're planning to cook the pasta immediately, 30 minutes of drying will allow the dough to set up correctly. To store them, dry them until they are stiff—about 8 hours—then put them in a plastic container until you're ready to cook them.

When you first see your own homemade pasta, you may be a bit put off by how rough it looks, but after a few batches of fresh, noodles from a box will start to look like mass-produced plastic cutouts. That's the moment you can call yourself a real artisan.

And the salt? It's for the water you boil the pasta in.

Basic Egg Noodles

If a boiled and shaped piece of dough made from flour and water is where noodle cuisine starts, then a boiled and shaped dough of flour, eggs, and water is a natural second step. The person who first added an egg to noodle dough and their logic for doing so is lost to history. Perhaps they wanted to share a hard-to-find protein source among a large group of dough eaters, or maybe it was some sort of happy accident. However it happened, it was obvious that this added ingredient made noodles with a more tender texture, a beautiful golden color, and more nutrition.

Egg noodle recipes are found all over the world, and they generally follow this basic formula.

1. Combine the flour and eggs in a large bowl. Mix until a dough forms, first with a wooden spoon, and then with your hands. If the mixture is too liquid, add flour, 1 tablespoon at a time, until it can be formed into a kneadable ball. If the mixture is too dry, add water, 1 tablespoon at a time, until the dough is soft enough to knead.

2. Sprinkle some flour on a flat surface and knead the dough. After about 5 minutes, it will be springy and elastic with gluten; this is the bread stage. For great noodles, you need to go beyond the bread stage and knead until the dough holds the shape you form it into without springing back, about 10 minutes.

MAKES 4 SERVINGS

2 cups flour* + flour for kneading

2 eggs

*While it must be wheat flour, you can use unbleached all-purpose, durum semolina, or a mixture of half all-purpose and half whole wheat.

3. Wrap the dough in a kitchen towel or plastic wrap and let it rest for at least 30 minutes. This gives the flour grains a chance to fully absorb the water.

At this point, the dough is ready for rolling, cutting, and drying for use in your chosen recipe (follow instructions at Basic Noodles, page 21). Or you could just roll the dough into thin sheets, cut the sheets into noodles, let them dry for 30 minutes or so, boil them up for 3 minutes, and serve them with a pat of melted butter.

Variation: In northern Italy, chefs make an even richer version of egg noodles by using only yolks. To do this, substitute 2 yolks for each egg. This dish, known as *tajarin*, is served with butter, grated Parmesan, and (when possible) fresh truffle shavings.

A BIT OF COLOR

ADAPTED FROM *A WORLD OF DUMPLINGS*

In adding color to your noodles, the basic ingredients are spinach leaves for green and carrot for orange. Here are the recipes:

FOR GREEN:
1 cup wilted or thawed frozen chopped spinach leaves

FOR ORANGE:
1 cup carrot pieces, boiled until fork-tender

Combine either ingredient (but not both together!) in a blender with 1 cup of water. Purée until you have a smooth liquid. Substitute this for water in any wheat dough recipe.

You can make yellow pasta doughs too: add one teaspoon of ground turmeric for each cup of flour before adding any liquids and then proceed as usual.

BOILED AND DRAINED: COOKING PASTA THE RIGHT WAY

Pasta is easy enough to cook, and yet we cooks ruin it so often. What's going on here? The principle is simple enough: you put it in boiling water and cook until it becomes tender enough to eat. You then drain it and either eat it right away or incorporate it into your dish.

Here's the drill:

1. You don't need a huge amount of water, but you do need enough. Four quarts per pound is good. Too little and it will stick; too much and you'll waste lots of energy and time bringing the water to a boil.

2. Salt the water properly. Use one tablespoon per quart—coarse sea salt if possible, with kosher salt a perfectly good second choice. The salt penetrates the pasta while it's cooking and develops flavors.

3. *Boiling water* means just that. Water so hot that big bubbles are coming up to the top and bursting continuously. Throughout the cooking process, keep the water as hot as you can without it boiling over.

4. Stir the pasta enough so that it doesn't clump together. This means at least fifteen seconds of stirring right after you add the pasta to the pot and at least a few stirs a minute until you're ready to drain it.

5. For store-bought dry pasta, pay attention to the cooking time offered on the package and shorten it by 1 or 2 minutes. For some reason, manufacturers are afraid of consumers undercooking their products. Pasta intended for a baked dish should be boiled even less—and in some cases not at all. If you are using fresh pasta, the cooking time will be very short; don't walk away. Time it carefully and get it on the plate quickly.

6. Drain promptly. Don't let the noodles sit in the cooking water. Pasta destined to be under sauce should be drained and dressed quickly. Cooked pasta should be rinsed only if it's going to be served cold. Recipes in this book will specify when rinsing is necessary.

THE PASTA TOSS TEST

MY FAVORITE 16TH-CENTURY ITALIAN FOOD WRITER, Cristoforo da Messisbugo, wrote that pasta "should be cooked long enough to say a short prayer." Good advice for those who pray while cooking. Today, though, we all say al dente, which means "at teeth" in Italian and is somehow mistakenly understood as "undercooked." There's some sense to this. If pasta is so flabby that it doesn't offer any resistance when you bite into it, it won't have any taste, either. The problem is testing it properly.

I've watched all kinds of people, from elderly Italian ladies to Japanese teenagers, cook spaghetti, and everybody seems to use the same method to test for doneness—they taste it. The method seems reliable enough; the only problem might come from being indecisive or having a huge appetite and eating too much of it during testing.

Is there any other way? What about the method of grabbing a strand and throwing it at the wall? If it sticks, it's ready, if it doesn't, it needs more cooking. Presumably, if it's overcooked it will fall apart in your hand before you can give it a proper hurl.

I thought that the practice of spaghetti throwing began with a 1970s TV cooking show called *The Romagnolis' Table*. I clearly remember a scene that began with throwing pasta at the ceiling and devolved into the Romagnolis throwing pasta at each other. I found an earlier reference, a book called *You Can Cook If You Can Read* (Viking Press, 1946; no relation to today's website of the same name) and figured that there must be some earlier origin. I couldn't imagine pre-1946 Italians doing the throw test; it would be too wasteful. Or would they just peel the thrown strand off the wall and toss it back into the pot?

Did the whitewashed stucco of Italian homes and the painted drywall of America have the same pasta-adherence properties? There was no practical way for me to find out. Nobody I knew in Italy tossed their pasta (at least while I was watching). I could test it at home, though. My New Jersey condo could—for this purpose, at least—be considered typically American and would be a perfect venue for pasta throwing. It was time to try it.

My first chance came when I was testing the pasta for the Albanian spaghetti recipe on page 237. I pulled two strands out of the pot at the same moment and tasted one; it wasn't quite cooked. Then I tossed the other at a painted drywall surface. It didn't stick.

This opened up a strange possibility: the chance that tossing strands of spaghetti at a wall was in fact a reliable way to determine if they were done. Did this method actually have merit? It wasn't supposed to work; the experiment was supposed to have given me the opportunity to fill this page with snark—to make silly comments about old wives' tales and 1970s cooking shows.

Two minutes later, when it was time to test again, I could see my whole noodle-cooking life flash before my eyes. I was reliving all those times I made fun of people who suggested that pasta tossing was the right way to go. The suspense was unbearable.

Once again, I tasted a strand and threw the other. It was cooked perfectly and stuck to the wall. Dubiosity flooded my mind . . . nay . . . it enveloped my entire body. My toes didn't believe it and the hair on my head was skeptical too. The strand of spaghetti stayed stuck to the wall as if mocking all of my modernity, my sophistication, and my vast culinary knowledge.

I thought of visiting my wife's cousins in Italy, offering to make them a pot of spaghetti as a thank-you for putting me up, and then throwing strands at their whitewashed stucco walls—to test the validity of pasta throwing in a traditional setting. I could just hear the cousins talking to my wife. "So this is what they pay your husband to do? And you resent the way our government gives out money?" Luckily, my shame was accompanied by restraint and I made no travel plans.

In the end, and even though I seemed to have learned something, I didn't change my pasta-testing technique. Like Messisbugo, I say a short prayer and, just to make sure, I taste a strand or two. After all, the wall can't tell you if you need to add more salt.

SOAKED AND DRAINED: PREPARING RICE NOODLES THE RIGHT WAY

Smooth, brittle, and with the look of white Plexiglas, dry rice noodles represent a whole new world to most American cooks. Unlike noodles made from wheat, they need no cooking to be brought from dry to edible. Instead, in most cases, a simple soaking will do the job.

1. Find a bowl that's about two to three times the volume of the noodles and put the noodles in the bowl.

2. Cover with hot tap water (100–115 degrees is fine), then let the noodles soak for 5 minutes. After that, give them a few stirs and try to pull them apart every 3 minutes or so until they're tender. This will take about 20 minutes for fine noodles and longer for thicker. The thickest rice noodles can take 40 minutes or more.

3. When the noodles are tender, drain them. Give them a rinse in cold water, and drain them again. They should be able to stand about 30 minutes before they become too sticky to use.

If you try to speed things up with boiling water, the noodles will soften much faster, but they'll get unpleasantly mushy too. I warned you!

There's an exception; if you're making a cold rice noodle salad like *bún chay* (page 150), you'll want to either soak them in boiling water (as described in the recipe) or dunk the soaked noodles in boiling water for no more than 15 seconds. Follow that with a rinse in cold water and then let them drain until you use them—as quickly as possible, of course.

And if you're among the lucky few who can get fresh rice noodles? I find that these are at their best for frying and salads with a quick 15 seconds in boiling water, a cold rinse, and a quick drain. In a soup, do nothing—just make sure the broth you pour over them is piping hot. They'll be fine.

WHERE GLUTEN LURKS

Gluten is a complex mixture of proteins and starches that helps many grain-based foods bind together. It's what gives a great noodle its chew. If you are sensitive to gluten—as many people all over the world are—I encourage you to choose packaged noodle products that are specifically labeled "gluten free." Do *not* assume that because it doesn't have wheat, it doesn't have gluten. Strive to become one of those people who read every label in the supermarket, and when you find products that work for you, the recipes here will be waiting and ready.

PART I
AMERICAN NOODLE

THE UNITED STATES

Amish-Style Chicken Pot Pie

∾

How did Amish-Style Chicken Pot Pie get from the dish presented here to that frozen-in-a-foil-pan thing we've all come to know and (sometimes) love? The supermarket item is so ubiquitous, it may have hijacked the name, but this is the authentic Amish classic.

1. Cut the dough into 1 x 3-inch strips, place them on parchment or other nonstick paper, and let them dry a bit while you cook the chicken stew.

2. Put the chicken, salt, pepper, and water in a pot over high heat and bring to a boil. When the water boils, reduce the heat to medium-low and simmer, covered, until the chicken is cooked, about 20 minutes.

3. Bring the chicken back to a boil over high heat and add the celery, onion, carrot, and potato. Let boil, uncovered, for 1 minute. Then reduce the heat back down to medium-low and simmer uncovered until the potatoes are tender and the liquid has evaporated by at least a third, about 30 minutes.

4. Mix in the green peas, parsley, and noodles, and cook, stirring occasionally, until the peas are tender and the noodles are done, about 5 minutes.

Serve hot.

MAKES 4 SERVINGS

1 recipe Basic Egg Noodles (page 23) rolled to the 3 setting of your pasta machine (between $\frac{1}{16}$- and $\frac{1}{8}$-inch thick)

2 pounds boneless chicken thighs and/or breasts, cut in strips

1 teaspoon salt

1 teaspoon freshly ground pepper

6 cups water

1 cup chopped celery

1 cup chopped onion

1 cup chopped carrot

1 cup chopped potato

1 cup green peas (frozen are okay)

2 tablespoons chopped parsley

MAKES 2 SERVINGS

4 cups chicken broth

2 cups water

2 tablespoons grated fresh ginger

1 tablespoon soy sauce

1 cup chopped Spam

1 cup sliced carrot

½ cup green peas (frozen are okay)

¼ cup chopped scallions

8 ounces fresh ramen or lo mein noodles (find these at Asian grocery stores), cooked, rinsed, and drained

Hawaiian-Style Noodles in Soup with Spam: *Saimin*

If you're not a Pacific Islander, you might not share the region's respect for Spam, the canned pork product that's stable enough to last though a typhoon and adds a bit of unctuous porkyness to anything you cook it with.

1. Put the chicken broth in a large pot along with the water, the ginger, and the soy sauce and bring to a boil over high heat.

2. When the broth is boiling add the Spam and carrot, reduce the heat to medium-low, and simmer covered, stirring occasionally, until the carrot becomes tender, about 15 minutes.

3. Mix in the green peas and scallions, give the mixture a few stirs, remove from the heat, and set aside.

4. To assemble, put a portion of the noodles at the bottom of a large soup bowl and ladle half the broth/Spam mixture over it. Use the rest for a second serving. Separate the noodles with a fork to help coat them with broth.

Serve right away.

MAKES 6 SERVINGS

½ cup unsalted butter
+ butter for the baking dish

1 teaspoon dried oregano

½ teaspoon dried chile flakes

1 teaspoon salt

1 teaspoon freshly ground pepper

½ cup all-purpose flour

3 cups whole milk

8 ounces cheddar cheese, cut in
small pieces (about 2 cups)

4 ounces mozzarella cheese, cut in
small pieces (about 1 cup)

¼ cup grated Parmesan cheese

1 pound macaroni, cooked for half
the recommended time and drained*

¼ cup unseasoned dry breadcrumbs

*Most people will use elbow
macaroni, but the traditional tube
shape is an interesting variation.
You can really surprise people by
using pasta not normally associated
with this dish, like shells or spirals.

Baked Macaroni and Cheese

Baked? Yes, not packaged and then cooked in a saucepan, but baked. Macaroni and cheese began as a casserole. Even though most of us know the boxed variety as an American cousin of instant ramen (page 98), macaroni and cheese wasn't always instant. Indeed, back in the day, when macaroni itself had not yet been bent into elbows and cheddar cheese wasn't bright orange, this was a real home-cooked dish.

1. Preheat the oven to 325 degrees and have a wire whisk ready.

2. Melt the butter in a large pot over medium heat and mix in the oregano, chile flakes, salt, and pepper. Stir until all are coated with the melted butter, about 1 minute.

3. With continuous whisking, slowly add the flour. It will quickly turn into a paste. Keep cooking the paste, stirring frequently, until it begins to turn tan, about 5 minutes.

4. Whisk in the milk, 1 tablespoon at a time. It must be added slowly enough to be absorbed by the flour. Wait until the flour expands and absorbs the liquid milk in the pot before adding more. Expect this step to take about 15 minutes.

5. Mix in the cheddar, mozzarella, and Parmesan, remove the pot from the heat, and mix in the cooked macaroni. Set aside.

6. Butter a 9 x 13-inch baking dish and add the macaroni and cheese mixture. Cover with an even layer of breadcrumbs and bake until the breadcrumbs are deeply browned and the cheese is bubbling, about 60 minutes.

Let rest for 15 minutes and serve warm.

YES, YOU CAN! IMPROVING INSTANT MAC AND CHEESE

I AM VERY SUSPICIOUS OF PEOPLE who live in the modern world, have modest incomes, yet claim never to eat any convenience foods, ever. I'll try not to stare and ask something like, No coffee to go? No instant noodles? No fast food? The rest of us need to share notes, though. Haven't we all come face to face with prepackaged macaroni and cheese, America's most iconic poverty food? Surely you've downed it at one time or another, on a camping trip or in a dorm room. Instant mac and cheese is a great American unifier. Here are some improvements.

1. The luxury move. Add truffle oil—the cheaper the better—to a batch of instant mac. Mix in 2 tablespoons of truffle oil at the same time you're adding the cheese powder. Truffle oil has a way of giving a woodsy, foresty aroma to whatever you put it on; either that or it makes the dish taste like old sneakers. Sometimes it's both; the scent of the forest and the essence of gym shoe combine in a good way.

2. Far more sensible are carrots and peas. Measure out a cup from those bags of bulk frozen. You keep them around for moments like this, don't you? Add them along with the cheese powder while you're cooking.

3. How about the most fashionable poverty food of them all, bacon? Never add raw; instead, mix in 1 cup of chopped, cooked bacon as the last step before serving. While I don't endorse it myself, precooked chopped bacon would work nicely, although frying some real bacon in a skillet gives a much better result.

4. A small can of tuna will add a nice touch and a bit of badly needed protein. Canned salmon works here too. In either case, just drain the can and add the contents to the macaroni and cheese mixture when it's just about finished cooking. Will this work with other kinds of canned meat and fish? A definite no for sardines or oysters, and a double no if they're smoked. Spam chopped into little pieces and browned in a skillet can work, although you'd be left with the same problem you have with bacon: two dirty pots to make a cheap, instant meal.

5. Other vegetables can be good too. Once again, though, you have to be certain you're not doing more work than you would to make a far more complicated and satisfying dish. A cup of frozen chopped spinach added at the same time as the cheese powder can be great. Sliced fresh mushrooms (you can buy them prepped this way in the supermarket) added at that same moment will also do the trick.

Can you mix things up? Sure; carrots, peas, and bacon work well together, as do bacon and mushrooms. Be forewarned: truffle oil doesn't really go with any of the other add-ins. And canned tuna is pretty limited too. Okay, maybe canned tuna and peas. Maybe.

Traditional Macaroni Salad

Some of us know this dish only as a side in delis, airline lunches, or mass-feeding emporiums. If that's the case for you, I'm sorry to hear it. It's much better than you might think.

1. Combine the mayonnaise, mustard, vinegar, and sugar in a small bowl and mix well. Make sure the sugar hasn't lumped; it should be properly dissolved. Set aside.

2. Combine the onion, celery, pepper, carrot, cooked macaroni, and any optional additions you've chosen in a large bowl and toss a few times.

3. Mix in the mayonnaise and mustard mixture and season with the salt and pepper. The macaroni and vegetables must be evenly coated; this takes a bit of work. Let the mixture sit in the refrigerator for at least 1 hour before serving.

Serve chilled and store in the refrigerator.

MAKES 4 SERVINGS

1 cup mayonnaise

¼ cup spicy brown mustard

2 tablespoons cider vinegar

¼ cup white sugar

½ cup chopped red onion

1 cup chopped celery

1 cup chopped red bell pepper

½ cup grated carrot

1 pound elbow macaroni, cooked for 2 minutes less than called for, rinsed, and drained

1 teaspoon salt

1 teaspoon ground white pepper

OPTIONAL ADDITIONS

½ cup chopped dill or sweet pickle (one or the other, not both!)

1 cup chopped cooked bacon and/or ham

MAKES 4 SERVINGS

¼ cup butter

¼ cup olive oil

1 teaspoon salt

1 teaspoon ground white pepper

5 cloves garlic, crushed
but not chopped

2 tablespoons finely
chopped Italian parsley

1 pound spaghetti,
cooked and drained

Spaghetti Bordelaise

Spaghetti Bordelaise is a New Orleans classic. It has nothing to do with Bordeaux at all and somehow references Italian with its use of spaghetti and olive oil. In the end, though, it becomes its own unique self.

1. Melt the butter in a large skillet over low heat. Mix in the olive oil, salt, pepper, and garlic. Cook, stirring frequently, until the garlic has become tender, about 15 minutes. Discard the garlic pieces.*

2. Remove the oil mixture from the heat and mix in the parsley.

Toss with the cooked spaghetti and serve right away.

*Better yet, spread the softened garlic on toast for an incredible treat.

Chicken Noodle Soup

MAKES 8 SERVINGS

¼ cup olive oil

2 teaspoons salt

1 teaspoon freshly ground pepper

2 teaspoons dried oregano

1 teaspoon dried thyme

1 large chicken, cut in pieces
(about 2–3 pounds)

2 cups chopped onion

1 cup chopped carrot

1 cup chopped potato

1 cup chopped celery

4 quarts water

3 bay leaves

1 cup green peas
(frozen are okay)

8 ounces egg noodles, dry

Tyler Cowen, the noted Washington, DC, area food blogger, has written that "all food is ethnic food," and every time I see that quote I nod enthusiastically in agreement. That is, until it comes to chicken noodle soup. Sure, people have been putting chicken and noodles together in soup for a very long time; it's just that the soup as we Americans know it today was invented by canning companies less than a hundred years ago. Not as a new food, but as a sort of averaging of the various ethnic varieties out there.

The result is predictable. Chicken noodle soup took hold in our national psyche, became a favorite, and with no traditional or official version, went off in way too many directions. I have seen chicken noodle soups that seem more suited to horror anthologies than cookbooks. If you've wound up opening a can once too often in search of the old-fashioned stuff, your remedy is right here: chicken noodle soup made from scratch.

1. Put the olive oil, salt, pepper, oregano, and thyme in a Dutch oven over medium-high heat and cook and stir until the spices are coated with the oil, about 1 minute.

2. Add the chicken parts and cook, stirring occasionally, until they're browned on both sides, about 15 minutes. Remove and set aside.

3. Without cleaning or even wiping out the Dutch oven, reduce the heat to medium-low and mix in the onion. Cook, stirring frequently, until the onion has turned translucent, about 15 minutes.

4. Mix in the carrot, potato, and celery and cook, stirring occasionally, until they start to become tender, about 15 minutes.

5. Raise the heat to high, add the water and bay leaves, and bring to a boil. Let boil for 1 minute. Reduce the heat to medium-low and return the browned chicken to the pot. Simmer covered, stirring occasionally, until the meat is very tender and falling off the bone, about 60 minutes. Once again, remove the chicken from the pot and set aside.

6. Pick the meat off the chicken bones and return meat to the pot, discarding the bones. Then mix in the peas and noodles and cook, stirring occasionally, until the noodles are tender, about 5 minutes. Serve hot and right away.

Note: If you're making this—or any—noodle soup ahead of time, don't add the noodles themselves until you're about ready to serve it. Otherwise, they'll keep on absorbing liquid and you'll wind up with a soggy noodle stew.

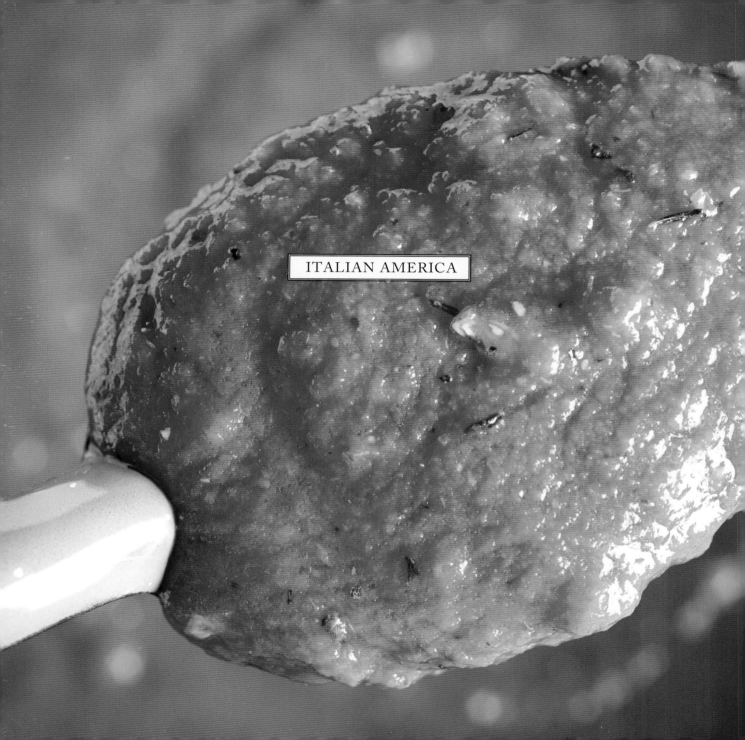

ITALIAN AMERICA

Pasta Primavera

MAKES 4 SERVINGS

Imagine you're back in the 1970s and fancy restaurants in places like Manhattan and Beverly Hills suddenly have to serve their very fussy and not very gastronomically informed clientele something with loads of vegetables. Somehow, they created a classic—gave it a snazzy Italian name—and it trickled down from those star-studded places to local Italian restaurants to diners. And since this was decades before the local-foods movement, sharp-eyed readers will notice that the dish has nothing at all to do with *primavera*—Italian for spring.

3 tablespoons butter

2 tablespoons crushed and finely chopped fresh garlic

1 teaspoon salt

½ teaspoon freshly ground pepper

½ cup red bell pepper strips

1 cup chopped broccoli

1 cup chopped yellow zucchini

1 cup snow peas

1 cup chopped fresh tomato

½ cup peas (frozen is fine)

½ cup heavy or whipping cream

¼ cup grated Parmesan cheese

¼ cup fresh basil leaves

1 pound pasta, cooked and drained*

*Spaghetti or linguine are traditional, but larger shapes work fine too. For an ultra-fancy touch, use fresh egg noodles; for the health-conscious crowd, use whole wheat pasta.

1. Put the butter, garlic, salt, and pepper in a skillet over medium heat and cook and stir until the butter melts and the garlic starts to turn translucent, about 10 minutes.

2. Mix in the pepper strips, broccoli, zucchini, snow peas, and tomato, and cook, stirring occasionally, until the vegetables become tender, about 15 minutes.

3. Add the peas and cream and stir until the vegetables are well-coated, about 1 minute.

4. Mix in the Parmesan and basil and stir until the leaves are well coated and the cheese is evenly distributed, about 1 minute. Remove from heat.

5. Toss with the cooked pasta and serve right away.

CUISINE OF DREAMS: WHERE ITALIAN AMERICA BEGINS

WE AMERICANS ARE DEEPLY IN LOVE with the notion of a romantic immigrant experience. This is the picture that comes to mind: those 19th-century Italians hopped off the boat, were thrilled by the cheap meat, and cooked up big pots of spaghetti and meatballs to celebrate. It's a scene that's been depicted in a thousand movies. It sure wasn't reality, though.

Instead, when those immigrants set foot on American soil, they began to work almost immediately. In the cities, sweatshop conditions made the notion of a lunch break impossible. Factory bosses would wash the work tables with gasoline in order to make sure that nobody ate on the job. In the mines and mills of Pennsylvania and West Virginia, lunch was whatever could be carried in a tin box during a twelve-hour shift.

No wonder they wanted huge meals at home!

Domenica Marchetti, an author whose work often takes her right up to the fine line between Italian and Italian American cuisine, told me that she saw Italian American cooking as "a cuisine of memory." In other words, dishes prepared not as they'd been taught, but rather, as people who weren't likely cooks themselves remembered them.

How could this be?

Imagine being sent alone by boat to America, arriving eventually in rural West Virginia. Your trip began in an equally rural Italian hill town where you were too poor to go to school and unable to find work. Were you ten? Twelve? Certainly no older! Could you read? Did the small-town dialect of Italian you spoke even exist in written form?

Things weren't any better for the girls who were sent over—almost always alone—to marry those boys. In a typical scenario, the guys would be working from dawn until dusk in the mines or factories while their wives struggled to cook, clean, and parent. The girls may have known how to make their hometown favorites, but could they describe the key ingredients to shopkeepers? Or

read the labels on packages? It wasn't that easy.

As time wore on, these families created a cuisine. Some ingredients like salt fish and capers were shelf-stable enough to buy as imports. And there were vegetables like peppers and eggplants that thrived in American soil. Pork didn't exactly taste the same as it did back in Italy, but it was cheap in America. Residents of the tenements of New York or Boston could get away for a day to dig clams. Soon, more items became available. Olive oil, for one. Maybe not the pure stuff we buy today, but a blend with a distinct flavor. Then espresso coffee, sea salt, and dried pasta. Immigrants created a cuisine using Italian ingredients, but not exactly Italian. Maybe their memories weren't that clear, and cooking techniques didn't easily transfer from Italian to American climes, but oh, did they cook!

Whatever could be incorporated into meals was. Shannon Tinnell, a food and folkways writer from West Virginia, tells of Appalachian favorites like poke and ramps making their way into traditional Italian soups and sauces. Immigrants converted *La Vigilia,* the simple meal of fish on Christmas Eve, into the Feast of the Seven Fishes, almost a holiday in its own right.

By the mid-20th century, children of Italian ancestry on both sides of the Atlantic were receiving better educations than a century before and were able to correspond with each other in standardized Italian. (Just before World War I, there were more than 40 Italian-language newspapers in West Virginia alone.) What both cultures shared was a near-worship of Grandma's cooking and the painful memory that preindustrial Italy had not been able to feed itself sufficiently.

Cooking in Italy is perhaps more a cuisine of dreams than of memories. It's what the great-grandparents of fourth-generation Italian Americans ate on the rare occasions when there was enough food to prepare whole meals. A fistful of pasta with a couple of stalks of broccoli might have been a typical meal

for the Italian country folk who sent their sons and daughters to America, but after Italy had its own industrial revolution and everybody could afford to eat, they did things a bit differently.

For Italians who had suffered through deprivation, every meal became a wedding banquet. A weeknight dinner at home might have four or five courses. Sunday lunches would go on for hours, and no meal was so informal that it could be served on paper plates. In Italy, eating was a ritual and a religion rolled into one. When Italy joined the Common Market and its own industries began to boom, everybody started consuming veal, artichokes, even truffles.

In the modern era—a time when Italian farmers and factory workers visit Florida's Disney World and American descendants of immigrant coal miners vacation in Tuscan hill towns—all of us have dreams and memories when it comes to food. Immigrant cuisines all seem to tell a familiar story—about hardworking people pulling themselves out of poverty and fixing themselves something good to eat.

Poor Man's Pasta with Vegetables

MAKES 4 SERVINGS

There might not have been much else, but there was usually dry pasta, a bit of vegetable, some oil, and a few scrapings of cheese. For decades, Italian immigrants in coal country would call this a meal. Indeed, a shake of dried chile flakes would have been seen as a luxury.

1 pound dry pasta (big shapes like rigatoni and ziti work best)

2 tablespoons salt

1 pound broccoli florets

2 tablespoons olive oil

1 teaspoon freshly ground pepper

2 tablespoons grated Parmesan cheese

1. Add the dry pasta and salt to 6 quarts of boiling water. Reduce the heat to medium-low and let the pasta simmer until it's barely soft and about one-third cooked, about 3 minutes.

2. Mix in the broccoli and continue to cook until both the pasta and broccoli are tender, about 6 minutes. Drain and put in a large bowl.

3. Toss the pasta and broccoli with the oil, pepper, and Parmesan cheese and make sure that all are well-distributed in the bowl. Serve with a shake of dried chile flakes on the side.

MAKES 6 SERVINGS

3 tablespoons olive oil

1 tablespoon dried oregano

2 teaspoons dried thyme

¼ teaspoon dried rosemary

1 teaspoon dried chile flakes

1 tablespoon salt

2 teaspoons freshly ground pepper

3 cups chopped onion

3 tablespoons crushed
and chopped fresh garlic

1 pound ground pork*

2 cups red, yellow, and/or
green bell pepper strips*

6 cups canned crushed tomato

2 cups ricotta cheese

1 pound ziti pasta, cooked for half
the recommended time and drained

2 cups shredded mozzarella

½ cup grated Parmesan cheese

½ cup grated pecorino Romano cheese

Oil or oil spray for the baking dish

*Ground pork and bell pepper strips,
my secret weapons! A tip: You can
find precut bell pepper strips in the
freezer section of the supermarket.

Baked Ziti

What would an informal dinner party be without a tray of baked ziti? Red sauce, gooey cheese, and of course those big pieces of pasta, the ziti. You better get started though; whipping up a batch of baked ziti means that hungry people must already be waiting for you.

1. Put the oil in a large skillet over high heat and mix in the oregano, thyme, rosemary, chile flakes, salt, and pepper. Cook and stir until the spices are coated with oil, about 2 minutes.

2. Reduce the heat to medium and mix in the onion and garlic. Cook, stirring frequently, until the onion is translucent, about 15 minutes.

3. Mix in the ground pork and cook, continuing to stir frequently, until the meat is browned, about 30 minutes. Use a wooden spoon to break the pieces of pork into the smallest possible size.

4. Preheat the oven to 375 degrees.

5. Mix the bell pepper strips and tomato into the meat mixture and cook, stirring occasionally, until the pepper strips are tender, about 10 minutes.

6. Mix in the ricotta and stir frequently until the cheese is combined with the sauce, about 5 minutes. You may have to use a wooden spoon to break it up a bit. Remove from the heat.

7. Oil a 9 x 13-inch baking dish and spread a thin layer of the tomato sauce on the bottom of it, cover with a layer of ziti, and cover that with a layer of mozzarella, Parmesan, and pecorino.

8. Repeat step 7 until you have filled the pan. Usually, this is three layers.

9. Sprinkle any remaining mozzarella, Parmesan, and pecorino on top of the ziti and sauce mixture.

10. Bake until the cheeses melt and fully combine, about 60 minutes.

Remove from the oven and let stand for at least 15 minutes before serving.

MAKES 6 SERVINGS

2 tablespoons olive oil

1 teaspoon dried oregano

1 teaspoon dried thyme

1 teaspoon salt

½ teaspoon freshly ground pepper

½ teaspoon dried chile flakes

½ teaspoon ground cinnamon

1 pound ground beef

3 cups canned crushed tomato

1½ pounds spaghetti or other pasta, cooked and drained

Spaghetti and Meat Sauce American-Style

It's the sauce you got at school lunch and it's the sauce your friend's mom made. Its roots are Italian, the meat is beef, and the spirit? Give it a taste and see for yourself. And it doesn't have to be spaghetti; feel free to substitute any pasta shape you might have around the house.

1. Put the olive oil, oregano, thyme, salt, pepper, chile, and cinnamon in a large skillet over medium heat. Cook and stir until all the spices are coated with oil and there are no clumps, about 1 minute.

2. Add the beef and cook, stirring frequently, until the meat is browned, about 15 minutes. Use the back of a wooden spoon to

make sure it breaks down into small pieces. Big lumps might not brown or cook properly.

3. Mix the crushed tomato into the beef and spice mixture, reduce the heat to medium-low, and cook, stirring occasionally, until about a quarter of the liquid has evaporated and the raw tomato taste is gone, about 20 minutes. If at any point the sauce bubbles and splatters, reduce the heat to low.

Serve hot over the cooked pasta and top with grated Parmesan cheese.

MEATBALLS

I have seen whole cookbooks and restaurants devoted to meatballs. Indeed, they're a universal dish genre in themselves. Yes, I agree that meatballs are crucial to the Italian American cooking experience, and no, I don't feel the need to put a full recipe for them in this book. Instead, if you want meatballs with any of these dishes—or even by themselves—just buy mild Italian sausage meat, form it into balls, add it to your basic (page 101) or not exactly basic (page 61) tomato sauce, and simmer, stirring occasionally, over medium-low heat until they're cooked through, about 30 minutes; rare meatballs are never a hit. If the flavor of sausage meat is too strong for you by itself, mix it half and half with ground beef.

You want a separate serving of meatballs? Instead of simmering them in sauce, put them on a baking sheet and brush or spray them with olive oil. Then bake them at 400 degrees until they're nicely browned, about 30 minutes.

That's it.

Pappardelle with Tuna and Tomato Sauce

MAKES 2 SERVINGS

Today, the broad, flat noodles known as pappardelle are a luxury ingredient often found in fancy packaging. Long ago, though, they were made at home with flour from a big sack, and eggs laid by your own chickens. Add some canned tomato and cheap fish—canned tuna and anchovies—and you have the meal of choice for poor Italian American coal miners of a century ago.

1. Put the oil, anchovies, and oregano in a large skillet over medium heat and cook and stir until the anchovies have dissolved, about 3 minutes.

2. Add the garlic and cook, stirring occasionally, until the garlic browns at the edges, about 5 minutes.

3. Mix in the tomato and tuna, reduce the heat to medium-low, and use the back of a wooden spoon to break the tuna up into small pieces. Then simmer until the raw tomato taste is gone and the volume has reduced by a quarter, about 15 minutes.

4. Add the cooked pasta, toss until it's evenly coated with sauce, and remove from the heat. Serve right away.

Note: The sauce can be made in advance or prepared while the pasta water is coming to a boil.

2 tablespoons olive oil

3 anchovy fillets

1 teaspoon dried oregano

2 tablespoons crushed and chopped fresh garlic

1 cup canned crushed tomato

1 can tuna (about 5 ounces) packed in water, drained

½ pound pappardelle pasta, cooked and drained

MAKES 4 SERVINGS

¼ cup olive oil

10 anchovy fillets

½ teaspoon dried chile flakes

4 cloves garlic,
crushed and chopped

2 tablespoons capers,
rinsed and drained

1 cup unflavored dry breadcrumbs

1 teaspoon salt

½ teaspoon freshly ground
black pepper

1 pound spaghetti, perciatelli
or other long, thick pasta,
cooked and drained

Spaghetti with Anchovies and Breadcrumbs: *Pasta Ammuddicata*

With or without capers, this is a classic frugal, southern Italian dish. A few anchovies and a pinch of dried chile flakes bring enough flavor to season an entire pound of dry pasta and breadcrumbs too. It's a bit of magic.

1. Put the oil and anchovies in a large skillet or sauté pan over medium-low heat. Cook and stir until the anchovies have broken up and dissolved, about 3 minutes.

2. Mix in the chile flakes and garlic and cook, stirring occasionally, until the garlic has turned translucent, about 8 minutes.

3. Mix in the capers, breadcrumbs, salt, and black pepper and cook and stir until all the breadcrumbs are coated with the oil mixture and begin to toast, about 5 minutes. Remove from the heat.

4. Add the cooked pasta to the pan and toss until all pasta is evenly coated.

Serve right away.

Not-Exactly-Basic Tomato Sauce

Basic tomato sauce (page 101) may be authentically Italian, but this American version takes things a step further. It's the jazzed-up vegetarian tomato sauce that finds its way onto pasta all over the Italian food universe. Some Americans would call this marinara sauce, though more than a few Italian-food fanatics would dispute the name. I'll step away from that debate and do some cooking and eating.

1. Put the oil, oregano, thyme, bay leaves, salt, and pepper in a large pot over medium heat and cook, stirring, until the spices are coated with the oil, about 1 minute.

2. Mix in the onion, carrot, and garlic, reduce the heat to medium-low, and cook, stirring occasionally, until the onion is translucent and the carrot is very tender, about 30 minutes. Make sure you stir often enough to prevent the garlic from burning.

3. Mix in the tomato and grated cheese and continue to cook with occasional stirring until the raw taste is gone from the tomato and the flavors have combined, about 20 minutes.

Serve by spooning over any good cooked dried pasta. Don't overdo it—a few tablespoons of sauce per person is enough, trust me!

Note: This sauce freezes well and makes a great afternoon cook-ahead project.

MAKES 6 CUPS

¼ cup olive oil

1 tablespoon dried oregano

1 tablespoon dried thyme

2 bay leaves

1 teaspoon salt

½ teaspoon freshly ground pepper

1 cup chopped onion

1 cup chopped carrot

3 tablespoons crushed and chopped garlic

6 cups canned crushed tomato

2 tablespoons grated pecorino Romano cheese

MAKES 4 SERVINGS

3 tablespoons butter

8 cups sliced onion (Wait till you see how little is left in the end)

1 cup shredded carrot

1 teaspoon salt

1 teaspoon freshly ground pepper

1 pound spaghetti, cooked and drained*

*This sauce works well with larger pasta shapes like rigatoni or candele too.

Spaghetti with Caramelized Onions

Smothered and caramelized onion sauces are popular in Italy, but almost never show up in the United States. The recipe here began its life as an authentic Italian dish, and after many experiments, became this: basic, slow-cooked caramelized onions in all their deliciousness. It will also teach you what happens to onions when they cook for a long time—they shrink. You start with an awful lot, and in the end there's not much at all.

1. Put the butter in a large skillet over medium heat and cook, stirring, until it melts, about 2 minutes.

2. Reduce the heat to low, then add the onion and cook, stirring occasionally, until the onion becomes limp, about 90 minutes. Remember, time is your friend here! Any attempt to speed things up will leave you with a sauce that's burnt and bitter.

3. Mix in the carrot, salt, and pepper and cook, stirring occasionally, until the onions have turned a deep golden brown, about 2 more hours. If a pool of liquid forms at the bottom of the pan, increase the heat slightly to medium-low until it evaporates—then return it to low.

4. Toss with the cooked pasta.

Serve right away with freshly grated Parmesan cheese.

CHINESE AMERICA

Chicken Lo Mein

How much chicken lo mein have you consumed in your life? For me, the question would be easier to answer if I replied in tons rather than portions. Fifteen or twenty in airport terminals, a couple more at small-town Chinese American restaurants that were walking distance from roadside motels. Then there's all the chicken lo mein I had during lunch breaks back in the days I was employed in Manhattan. It could well be that this is America's most widely consumed noodle dish.

And why make it at home? Um . . . because it will almost certainly taste better than at the airport.

1. Combine the chicken, teaspoon of sugar, vinegar, wine, ¼ cup soy sauce, and cornstarch in a bowl. Mix well and let marinate in your refrigerator for at least 1 hour.

2. In a separate container, combine the 2 teaspoons of sugar, tablespoon of soy sauce, chicken broth, and sesame oil and mix well. Set aside.

3. Drain the chicken, discard the marinating liquid, and put a wok or very large skillet on high heat. Stir-fry the chicken until it's barely cooked through, about 2 minutes. Remove it from the pan and set aside.

MAKES 2 SERVINGS

8 ounces boneless chicken thighs, cut into strips

1 teaspoon sugar +
2 teaspoons sugar

2 tablespoons rice wine vinegar

1 tablespoon Chinese cooking wine

¼ cup soy sauce + 1 tablespoon soy sauce

1 teaspoon cornstarch

½ cup chicken broth

1 tablespoon sesame oil

2 tablespoons peanut oil

1 tablespoon crushed and chopped garlic

2 tablespoons minced fresh ginger

1 cup sliced fresh shiitake mushroom caps

½ cup shredded carrot

8 ounces dried lo mein noodles, or 12 ounces fresh, cooked and drained

¼ cup chopped scallion greens

1 teaspoon ground white pepper

4. With the wok (and the oil in it) still over high heat, stir-fry the garlic and ginger until the pieces start browning at the edges, about 2 minutes.

5. Mix in the mushrooms and carrot and stir-fry until the mushrooms are cooked through, about 3 minutes.

6. Mix in the cooked chicken, cooked noodles, and broth and soy sauce mixture. Toss until all the ingredients have combined, about 3 minutes.

7. Add the scallions and pepper and stir-fry until the scallions are tender, about 1 minute.

Serve right away.

STIR-FRYING

AS A COOKING TECHNIQUE, stir-frying is so common today, you might think it needs no more discussion. Like boiling, everybody knows what it is and has a sense of how it's done. This hasn't always been the case. Before World War II, there were no English-language terms for Asian cooking techniques at all. There were certainly Chinese cooks in America with a desire to write down their techniques and traditions in English, but not really much of an audience. American home cooks made what their moms taught them, and restaurant kitchens executed their chefs' instructions.

By the 1950s, though, things began to change. Soldiers returning from war told tales of foods that were as bizarre as they were delicious. Pizza, sushi, and who knows how many versions of fried noodles were suddenly a topic of conversation.

This was the audience that Dr. Buwei Yang Chao faced when she sat down to write *How to Cook and Eat in Chinese*. Stuck in Boston with a husband at Harvard and a world war cutting her off from her home in Taiwan, she was unable to practice medicine and looking for something to do. The result was her book; published in 1945, it was the first to accurately describe Chinese cooking techniques in English.

Before that time, the term *stir-fry* didn't exist, and the only people who knew what *braise* and *sauté* meant were graduates of French cooking schools or their staffs. Chao explains that "stir-frying is the most characteristic method of cooking in Chinese. This is when you really have to cook *in* Chinese, since the Chinese term *ch'ao* with its aspiration, lo-rising tone and all cannot be translated into English. Roughly speaking, *ch'ao* may be defined as a big-fire-shallow-fat-continual-stirring-quick-frying of cut-up material with wet seasoning. We shall call it 'stir-fry.'"

The first time I cracked open a copy of this book—in a study room at the New York Public Library—and read this passage, I felt chills running up my spine. This was the beginning of Asian home cooking in America. It would eventually lead to thirty-minute infomercials for hand-hammered woks, Asian sections in local supermarkets, and a whole subcategory of cooking literature devoted to this part of the world. No longer would American home cooks be limited to the food of Europeans. With this now-ubiquitous term, *stir-fry,* Chinese food—already the most cooked cuisine in American restaurants—could be made at home.

Chao's definition of stir-frying remains the best I've seen. Indeed, her reminder that "noodles should not be wound around your chopsticks like spaghetti on a fork" tells us about another long-forgotten American eating habit.

Let's take a look at the two main issues I've found with stir-frying at home: You need heat and lots of it. Experts try for a temperature of over 700 degrees, which can rarely be reached on home stoves. Five hundred degrees will do the job most of the time, though, and if you wait an extra minute before you start adding solid ingredients, most modern ranges will get you there.

The proper pan for stir-frying is the second point. Of course, purists will call for a wok. Fanatics will quarrel about the type of metal and the texture of the surface of the wok. For our purposes, though, the most important thing is having a pan big enough to hold all the ingredients without overloading. You should be able to keep the food inside in constant motion without spills or splashing. Woks are great for this. A skillet is fine, too, though, as long as you have one that's large enough.

Have I spilled all the secrets? I don't know . . . what I'm sure of is that you'll get real stir-fry if you start with a hot pan and keep the food moving. If there isn't actual stirring and frying, it's not really a stir-fry.

PART II
BIG NOODLE

CHINA

Cold Noodles with Sesame Paste

For some people, cold sesame noodles are the worst kind of left-over Chinese take-out. For an older generation, this dish was one of the earliest examples of the Sichuan revolution in American Chinese restaurants that so changed the notion of the cuisine in America a few decades ago. Yes, there are those who remember this dish as their first encounter with a Chinese cuisine that wasn't chop suey or egg foo young—a food that's vibrant, flavorful, and not fried.

1. Combine the sesame paste, peanut butter, soy sauce, rice wine vinegar, sesame oil, chile flakes, sugar, ginger, and garlic in a bowl with the ¼ cup water. Mix well so that all the ingredients form a smooth paste. If it's too thick, add water, 1 tablespoon at a time, until it's about the consistency of a good tomato sauce. Set aside for at least 1 hour to let the flavors combine. If you're making this recipe ahead of time, refrigerate the sauce.

2. Assemble the dish by tossing the sauce with the cooked noodles and garnishing with the scallion greens, cilantro, and sesame seeds.

Serve right away. (Do not let the noodles and sauce sit for any length of time before serving.)

MAKES 4 SERVINGS

½ cup Chinese sesame paste or tahini

2 tablespoons peanut butter

3 tablespoons soy sauce

2 tablespoons rice wine vinegar

1 tablespoon sesame oil

1 teaspoon dried chile flakes

1 tablespoon sugar

1 teaspoon crushed and chopped fresh ginger

2 teaspoons garlic, crushed and chopped

¼ cup water

4 servings cooked Chinese egg noodles, about 1½ pounds*

2 tablespoons chopped scallion greens

2 tablespoons chopped cilantro leaves

2 tablespoons sesame seeds

*You can argue for hours about what noodles are "best" for this dish. Chinese egg noodles—a classic egg pasta dough in long, thin strands—are authentic, but I've had even better luck with a pound of good spaghetti, cooked properly, then rinsed, drained, and tossed with a spoonful of sesame oil.

MAKES 4 SERVINGS

½ pound ground pork

1 teaspoon soy sauce + 1 tablespoon for the sauce

2 teaspoons cornstarch

1 tablespoon sesame oil + 1 tablespoon for the sauce

½ cup chicken broth

1 tablespoon Chinese black vinegar

1 tablespoon chopped garlic

2 teaspoons chopped ginger

1 tablespoon crushed peanuts

1 tablespoon toasted sesame seeds

2 tablespoons Sichuan pickled mustard greens

2 tablespoons chopped scallion greens

1 tablespoon Chinese sesame paste or tahini

1 tablespoon chile oil

2 tablespoons peanut oil

2 pounds fresh Shanghai noodles (find them in a Chinese supermarket), cooked, rinsed, and drained

Noodles with Meat Sauce: *Dan Dan Mian*

Dan dan mian is China's take on noodles topped with ground meat and sauce. Traditionally, this dish is served at room temperature—imagine it coming from a street stall or peddler. Those who want it as a hot dish should put the cooked noodles into the bowl without rinsing and toss with the sauce right away. No matter the temperature at which it's served, it's pork, noodles, and a zing of spice—a unique, earthy flavor; the soul of Sichuan.

1. Combine the pork, teaspoon of soy sauce, cornstarch, and sesame oil in a bowl and let marinate in the refrigerator for at least 60 minutes.

2. Combine the tablespoon of soy sauce, sesame oil, chicken broth, black vinegar, garlic, ginger, peanuts, sesame seeds, mustard greens, scallions, sesame paste, and chile oil in a bowl and mix well. Marinate in the refrigerator for at least 30 minutes. Stir well before using.

3. Put a wok or skillet over very high heat and add the peanut oil and marinated pork. Cook, stirring, until the meat is very well browned, about 5 minutes. Use a wooden spoon to break up the meat and make sure there are no clumps. Set aside.

4. Assemble the dish by first putting noodles in a serving bowl, then spoon some of the sauce over them. Finally, top with the pork.

Note: If you really want to impress your guests, top this dish with a fried egg. It's very authentic and almost unknown here in the States.

AT TEETH

SOME PEOPLE SAY that if you walk into a Chinese restaurant and it's filled with Chinese customers, that's a good sign. It might be, or the restaurant may have recently handed out discount coupons, or the patrons could all be ordering some banal dish that reminds them of home, like plain buns or noodles. The restaurant I walked into recently, in a strip mall in New Jersey, was packed with the right kind of crowd. Mostly Chinese, and eating like lunchtime had finally come. A tiny room packed with dumplings, buns, and noodles.

You ordered at the counter. There was a gringo menu that managed to list General Tso's Chicken twice, convincing me even more forcefully that the General served in the New Jersey National Guard. And there was another menu, divided on the front page into "Shanghai Dim Sum" and "Noodles and Other." I wondered when *dim sum* became English for "Chinese snack," and ordered noodles. Shredded Beef in Spicy Noodles Soup, to be precise.

And there it was, the sublime, perfect pasta moment. A heap of thick, rough-cut white noodles, real beef broth with the flavor of bones very much in evidence, a bit of shredded beef, a splash of chile oil, a few slices of jalapeño, a few more of red bell pepper, and a fistful—okay, the fist of a small woman full—of chopped coriander leaves. Not much at all, really.

In Italy, they say *al dente* to describe the mouth feel of great pasta. The phrase translates into English as "at teeth," and refers to the firmness of the cooked noodles. I found myself enjoying the chew of these Chinese noodles so much that I invoked this overused phrase; the noodles were perfectly al dente.

A few noodles, a spoonful of broth, then maybe a slice of that pepper. Repeat. Repeat until you're licking the bottom of the bowl. Would you win *Top Chef* with this dish? On one hand, perhaps the most challenging cooking skill it exhibited was the avoidance of instant. On the other, the chef had somehow elevated the simple processes of boiling bones in a pot and mixing flour and water into acts of genius.

I picked up the last scrap of noodle with my chopsticks and relished it as I exercised my jaw. Could I replicate this? Could I improve on it? Would I have to convince my wife and friends to visit a strip mall in Matawan so they could grasp the basics of noodle excellence? Back in my car, I realized that the bit of broth, beef, and pasta I'd just eaten had driven me into a near state of ecstasy.

A bowl of noodles followed by real joy.

Cantonese Stir-Fried Noodles with Beef: Chow Mein

MAKES 2 SERVINGS

Not just a classic Cantonese dish and not a relative of American chow mein, Beef chow mein is the subject of rock music's most famous noodle lyric. "I saw a werewolf with a Chinese menu in his hand, / Walking though the streets of Soho in the rain. / He was looking for the place called Lee Ho Fook's, / Going to get a big dish of beef chow mein." Even if you're not a Warren Zevon fan, and even if you're not a rock music fan, this is a great simple dish with beef, vegetables, and, most of all, crunchy fried noodles.

¼ cup soy sauce

2 tablespoons Chinese cooking wine

1 teaspoon sugar

1 tablespoon sesame oil

½ teaspoon cornstarch

8 ounces boneless beef sirloin or flank steak cut into thin strips

8 ounces fresh chow mein noodles, cooked, rinsed, and drained*

1 cup peanut oil

1 tablespoon finely chopped fresh ginger

2 tablespoons crushed and chopped fresh garlic

1. Combine the soy sauce, cooking wine, sugar, sesame oil, and cornstarch in a bowl. Mix well so that the sugar dissolves. Then add the sliced beef and toss until the meat is covered with the liquid. Refrigerate and let marinate for at least 30 minutes. Give it a few stirs every 30 minutes or so if you leave it for longer.

(Recipe steps and ingredients list continue on page 76.)

1 cup sliced fresh shiitake
mushroom caps

1½ cups Chinese broccoli
cut into 2-inch pieces

¼ cup chopped scallions

*You can buy fresh precooked
noodles at many Asian markets.
They're too oily for soup but
will work perfectly here.

2. Put a wok or large skillet over high heat and add the oil. When the oil is very hot, about 375 degrees, use your hands to form the cooked noodles into two flat pancakes and use a spatula to put them in the oil, one at a time. When the bottom of the noodle cake has browned, about 3 minutes, use a spatula to flip it over. When the noodles are browned on both sides, remove them from the oil and drain on a rack or paper towels.

3. Remove the excess oil from the pan and put the pan back on high heat. Add the ginger, garlic, and white pepper and cook, stirring, until the garlic starts to brown at the edges, about 2 minutes.

4. Drain the excess liquid from the marinating beef and mix the beef strips in with the garlic and ginger. Cook and stir until the beef starts to brown, about 3 minutes.

5. Mix in the mushroom slices and broccoli and cook, stirring, until the broccoli is tender and the mushrooms cooked through, about 5 minutes.

6. Mix in the scallions and cook and stir until they wilt, about 1 minute.

To assemble the dish, put the fried noodles on a serving plate and pour the stir-fried meat and vegetables over them. Serve right away.

Almost-Instant Fish Ball Noodle Soup

This soup requires nothing more than a few things you can buy at any Chinese grocery. Throw them together for something far more authentic and tasty than anything on offer at your local Chinese takeout. This recipe is per person. Multiply by desired number of servings to scale up.

1. Put the cooked noodles at the bottom of a serving bowl.

2. Bring water to a boil in a saucepan, then add the soup base powder and reduce the heat to a simmer.

3. Mix in the fish balls and cook, stirring occasionally, until they expand a bit, about 3 minutes.

4. Add the bok choy leaves and keep cooking until they wilt, about 1 minute.

5. Pour the broth/fish ball/bok choy mixture over the noodles in the serving bowl. Put the cilantro and sesame oil on top, give the whole thing one more stir, and serve right away.

MAKES 1 SERVING

4 ounces fresh Shanghai noodles, cooked, rinsed, and drained

2 cups water

2 teaspoons wonton soup base powder*

6 fish balls or shrimp-stuffed fish balls

1 head baby bok choy, separated into leaves

2 tablespoons chopped fresh cilantro leaves

½ teaspoon sesame oil

*You can make a better broth by combining one cup boiling water, one cup chicken stock, and one teaspoon wonton soup base.

MAKES 2 SERVINGS

2 tablespoons soy sauce

1 tablespoon sugar

1 tablespoon sesame oil

¼ teaspoon cornstarch

½ pound ground pork

3 tablespoons peanut oil

1 tablespoon minced
fresh ginger

2 tablespoons crushed
and chopped fresh garlic

2 tablespoons chopped fresh
hot red chile pepper

¼ cup shredded carrot

1 cup sliced dried or fresh
shiitake mushroom caps

6 ounces bean thread noodles,
soaked, and drained

2 tablespoons sliced
scallion greens

Bean Thread Noodles with Ground Pork: Ants Climb a Tree

No cuisine anywhere matches the Chinese when it comes to poetic names. This famous Sichuan dish has no ants or trees and requires no climbing. Chinese chefs whimsically described the bits of pork as looking like ants and the strands of rice noodle as tree branches. Remember, you don't have to share that vision in order to enjoy the dish.

And what are these bean threads? They're a noodle made from bean starch. They look just like rice noodles and are sold in the same section you would find rice noodles in most food markets.

1. Mix the soy sauce, sugar, sesame oil, and cornstarch together in a large bowl and add the ground pork. Mix together so that as much of the pork as possible comes in contact with the soy mixture. Let marinate in the refrigerator until the pork absorbs the sauce flavors; about 30 minutes.

2. Put the oil in a wok or large skillet over high heat and mix in the ginger, garlic, and chile pepper. Cook and stir until the ginger starts to brown at the edges, about 2 minutes.

3. Mix in the marinated pork, carrot, and mushroom and cook and stir until the meat has browned, about 5 minutes. Use the back of a wooden spoon to break the meat up into the smallest possible pieces (remember, this is Ants Climb a Tree, not Elephants Climb a Tree).

4. Add the noodles and toss until the meat, carrot, mushroom, and scallion greens are evenly mixed into them and the noodles are heated through, about 2 minutes.

Serve right away. Fire eaters will demand hot sauce on the side.

TAIWAN

Squid and Mushroom Potage

MAKES 2 BIG BOWLS

This is it, the thick soup that thins out in your bowl. A real Taiwanese flavor if there ever was one.

1. Soak the mushroom pieces in warm water for 30 minutes. Drain and set aside.

2. Put half the cooked noodles in each serving bowl. Then put half the sprouts and half the scallion over the cooked noodles.

3. Put the broth, soaked mushrooms, ham, celery, ginger, pepper, wine, vinegar, soy sauce, and salt together in a pot and bring to a boil for 1 minute.

4. Add the dissolved cornstarch to the boiling soup and give it a few quick stirs. It should thicken quickly. Lower the heat to medium.

5. While stirring, add the beaten eggs. They will cook quickly.

6. Add the squid rings and let the liquid simmer for 1 more minute. They should be just barely cooked through.

7. Pour the soup into the serving bowls and over the noodles. Add the sesame oil and toss to make sure the noodles are covered with soup.

Serve right away or the soup will become watery.

½ cup dried shiitake mushroom pieces

8 ounces fresh lo mein noodles, cooked, rinsed, and drained

½ cup mung bean sprouts

2 tablespoons chopped scallions

4 cups chicken broth

¼ cup chopped ham*

½ cup chopped celery

1 teaspoon minced fresh ginger

½ teaspoon ground white pepper

¼ cup Chinese cooking wine

3 tablespoons Chinese black vinegar

1 tablespoon soy sauce

¼ teaspoon salt

1 tablespoon cornstarch dissolved in ¼ cup water

2 eggs, beaten

1 cup squid rings

2 tablespoons sesame oil

*Try to get Chinese ham or country ham, but any ham steak will do.

¼ cup peanut oil

2 pounds beef shank including the big piece of bone in the center

1 pound boneless chuck steak cut into 1-inch cubes

¼ cup crushed and chopped fresh garlic

¼ cup chopped fresh ginger

3 whole star anise

5 whole dried red chiles

½ cup chopped scallions

¼ cup chopped Chinese pickled cabbage

½ cup soy sauce

½ cup Chinese cooking wine

8 cups water

2 cups baby bok choy, cut into long strips

1 pound thick, fresh wheat noodles (udon works well here), cooked and drained

Beef Noodle Soup: *Hong Shao Niu Rou Mian*

Is this the national dish of Taiwan? Well . . . that would certainly have to be a noodle soup of some sort, and this is the most legendary, a big bowl of red cooked beef and thick noodles that can be a quick lunch or a late dinner. Whatever time you choose to eat it, this is Taiwan's comfort food and well worth a try.

1. Put a large pot over medium heat and add the oil, beef shank, and chuck. Cook, stirring occasionally, until the meat is well browned, about 20 minutes. Set the meat aside but don't clean the pot. The flavor in the residue is important.

2. In the same pot you used to cook the meat, mix in the garlic, ginger, anise, chiles, scallions, and pickled cabbage and cook over medium-low heat, stirring frequently, until the garlic is tender and browning at the edges, about 15 minutes.

3. Increase the heat to high and add the browned meat, soy sauce, cooking wine, and water and bring to a boil. Let the mixture boil for 1 minute and reduce the heat to medium-low. Simmer covered, stirring occasionally, until the meat is tender, about 60 minutes. Shut off the heat and let cool for a few moments.

4. Strain the broth into another pot. Reserve the meat and discard the spices. Remove the cooked meat from the beef shins and chop the meat into small pieces. Return the meat to the soup and

discard the bone. Put the liquid back on medium heat and cook, stirring occasionally, until it's warmed up again, about 5 minutes.

5. Mix in the bok choy and cook, stirring occasionally, until tender, about 5 minutes.

6. To assemble the soup, put a heap of cooked noodles at the bottom of a serving bowl, then ladle the soup over it, making sure everybody gets plenty of beef and bok choy

Japanese Chicken Broth

MAKES 3 QUARTS

1 large chicken, about 2-3 pounds, cut in pieces*

1 to 2 pounds chicken feet and/or wings

1 piece fresh ginger, 3 inches long

4 quarts water

*To make 3 quarts of broth, you'll need a total of 5 pounds of chicken. If you see a deal on, say, thighs or necks, use them instead of the whole chicken. But don't forget the feet and/or wings!

With all the salt in Japanese seasonings, you'll get the best results with a completely salt-free broth. Remember: don't add salt. The miso will do that job for you. And this holds true with other recipes too. Salt in the broth makes it harder to salt the finished dish.

1. Put the chicken in a large pot (but don't yet add the additional feet and/or wings), cover with water, and bring to a boil. Let boil for 30 seconds, remove the chicken, and set it aside, discarding the water.

2. Return the chicken to the pot, add the chicken feet and/or wings, ginger, and 4 quarts of water, and simmer covered over medium-low heat. Give it a stir every 10 or 15 minutes.

3. After about 3 hours, the bones and meat will have separated and the meat will break up into tiny slivers. At this stage, strain the solids from the broth, returning the liquid to the pot. Then taste the broth. If it's too strong, add water, a cup at a time, until it tastes right. If it's too watery, return the pot to the stove and simmer uncovered until it's strong enough. Taste it every 20 minutes and don't forget to give it an occasional stir. It's ready when it tastes more like chicken than water.

Don't be surprised when the broth gelatinizes as it cools. This is normal; it will return to liquid form when heated. Store in the refrigerator or freezer.

MAKES 2 SERVINGS

1 tablespoon peanut oil

1 tablespoon crushed and chopped fresh garlic

1 tablespoon chopped fresh ginger

4 cups Japanese chicken broth (recipe page 87, or low sodium from the supermarket)

2 cups dashi broth

¼ cup mirin

1 tablespoon sugar

¼ cup soy sauce

8 ounces fresh lo mein or ramen noodles, cooked, rinsed, and drained

2 tablespoons sesame oil

3 tablespoons nori strips

2 hard-cooked eggs, peeled and cut in half

Noodles in a Soy Sauce Broth: *Shoyu Ramen*

Soy sauce broth is the most basic way to serve a bowl of ramen noodles. It's the cheapest item on the menu and therefore a favorite of students, cooks, and budget travelers. For a quick bowl of noodle soup, make it with supermarket broth. For something a bit more amazing, make the chicken broth from scratch.

1. Put the peanut oil, garlic, and ginger in a wok or large pot over high heat and cook, stirring, until the garlic starts to brown at the edges, about 3 minutes.

2. Add the chicken broth, dashi, mirin, sugar, and soy sauce and bring to a boil. After boiling for 1 minute, reduce the heat to medium-low, and let simmer until the garlic becomes tender, about 5 minutes. Then skim or strain the broth to remove the garlic and ginger pieces.

3. Put the cooked noodles in their serving bowls, cover with the soup, drizzle with the sesame oil, and sprinkle the nori strips over the top. Finally, garnish with the cooked eggs.

Serve piping hot and right away.

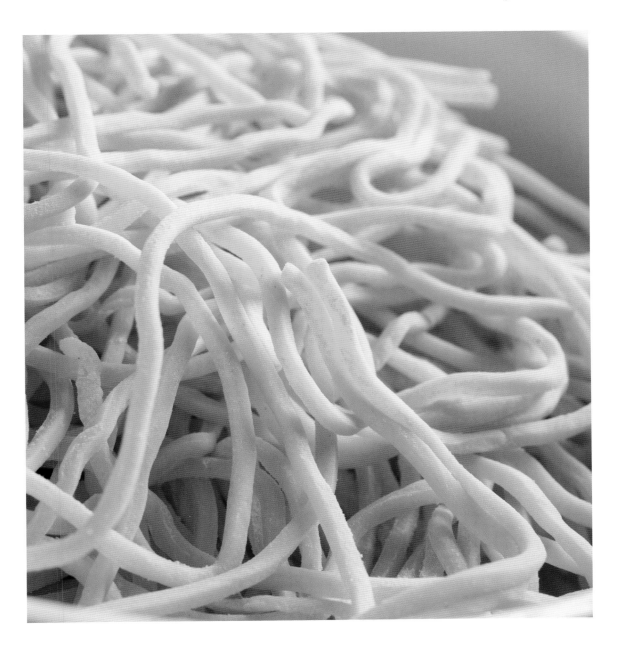

Noodles with Pork and Miso: *Miso Ramen*

Miso is one of the most Japanese of flavors. Made from fermented soybeans, miso broth is common in Japan, where it's found in every form from artisan to instant. It should come as no surprise that it's often combined with ramen noodles, Japan's most popular pasta.

1. Put the oil, garlic, ginger, and pork in a wok or sauté pan over medium heat and cook and stir until the meat begins to brown, about 5 minutes.

2. Mix in the bean sprouts, napa cabbage, and carrot and continue to cook, stirring occasionally, until the cabbage starts to become tender, about 3 minutes.

3. Add the chicken broth, sugar, soy sauce, sesame oil, and miso paste to the meat and vegetable mixture and bring to a simmer. You'll have to stir for at least 2 minutes to get the miso fully dissolved. The soup is ready when the miso is completely incorporated into the liquid.

4. Place a portion of cooked noodles in each serving bowl. Stir the soup one more time and ladle it over the cooked noodles. Make sure that all the noodles are wet with broth and not sticking together. Garnish with the scallions, sesame seeds, and fish cake.

Serve right away.

MAKES 2 SERVINGS

1 tablespoon peanut oil

1 clove garlic, crushed and chopped

1 tablespoon minced fresh ginger

¼ pound pork tenderloin, cut into thin strips

1 cup mung bean sprouts

1 cup napa cabbage, cut into thin strips

¼ cup shredded carrot

4 cups Japanese chicken broth (recipe page 87)

1 teaspoon sugar

1 tablespoon soy sauce

1 teaspoon sesame oil

3 tablespoons miso paste

8 ounces fresh ramen or lo mein noodles, cooked and drained

2 tablespoons chopped scallions

2 teaspoons sesame seeds

4 slices Japanese fish cake

THE SKINNY ON SOBA

I WAS A BIT RELUCTANT TO OFFER A RECIPE FOR SOBA, the popular Japanese buckwheat noodles. I figured that the traditions of soba making were upheld by stocky Japanese guys with big knives who honored hundreds of years of samurai noodle technique. And when I went to a soba-making demonstration and saw a few of them at work, I realized that I'd underestimated them. They might not have been as big-shouldered as I'd imagined, but their technique sent a shock wave of shame through me that will take at least a few reincarnations to erase.

The soba samurai had a process that flowed. They measured the flours, added a bit of water, and poof!—there was a perfectly formed puck of dough. Doughs made with only wheat flour will come together fairly easily; a bit of liquid does a fine job of binding, and your hands an equally fine job of kneading. Not so with buckwheat. However—and *however* is the key word here—if you bring the wheat, buckwheat, and water together in the right way, you'll get a perfectly workable dough. Otherwise you'll have to trash it and start again. Needless to say, the samurai didn't waste a single grain of flour.

The masters had a simple enough technique: they rubbed bits of moistened wheat/buckwheat mixture between their palms in a way that made them look like scheming bad guys in pirate movies. This formed the dough into sticky little pills that could be kneaded until

they stuck together. Given all this palm rubbing, the dough never started crumbling. It's a technique that works for the Italian dish *pizzoccheri* (page 108) too; it's pretty much the same dough, after all.

I held one advantage over the soba masters: a pasta machine. Each time one looked up at the crowd of viewers and made eye contact with me, I could imagine him thinking, "There's the jerk that cheats with that Italian steel-crank monstrosity! How dare you!" I silently fought back, reminding myself that these guys rolled with long wooden dowels that looked cool and required a lot of work. A good machine was no match for them. It's one thing to have wrists of steel and another to have steel itself.

I couldn't beat them on the dipping sauce. The real thing, with fish shavings, dashi, and Japanese rice wine, is the best. But then again, Italians put cooked cabbage and melted cheese on the exact same noodles, and that can be just as sublime. It's one of those great culinary mysteries.

MAKES 4 SERVINGS

2 cups buckwheat flour

1 cup all purpose flour
+ flour for kneading

1¼ cups water

1 teaspoon salt + 1 tablespoon
for the boiling water

Japanese Buckwheat Pasta: Soba

Make no mistake about it; buckwheat isn't wheat. It's a seed that can be ground into a flour that kind of looks like whole wheat, but not exactly. By itself, buckwheat is almost impossible to make into noodles because it lacks gluten, the stuff that holds them together. Therefore, some wheat flour is always added to do the job. Commercial soba has been found that's more than half wheat; very mild, but not all that different from udon or lo mein. In this recipe, we'll go with two-thirds buckwheat, enough for some real buckwheat flavor, but still kneadable.

1. Combine the buckwheat flour, wheat flour, and salt in a large bowl and add the water. Mix with a wooden spoon until a dough begins to form. If the mixture is too dry, add water, 1 tablespoon at a time, until a dough forms. If it's too moist, add wheat flour, 1 tablespoon at a time until you have something that resembles Play-Doh in texture.

2. Sprinkle flour on a flat surface and knead the dough until it's pliable enough to run through a pasta machine, about 5 minutes. Then let the dough rest for 20 minutes.

3. Run the dough through a pasta machine until you have thin, flat sheets. On my machine, the "4" setting is about where it should be. It takes 10 or 15 passes through thicker settings to reach this point. Alternatively, roll the dough flat with a rolling pin. This would take 5 to 8 minutes.

4. To cut the sheets of dough into strands of soba, use the fine noodle blades of a pasta machine or a very sharp knife. Sprinkle a bit of flour on the strands of soba to keep them from sticking. They can now be dried on a pasta rack if you're not using them immediately.

5. Cook the soba by putting it in boiling salted water for 2 minutes. For cold soba, rinse immediately in cold water, drain, and serve right away. For hot dishes, drain, add to broth or soup, and serve right away. (Do not cook the raw soba in soup or broth).

Note: Homemade soba will often break into smaller pieces because of the lack of gluten. Don't let this bother you. The flavor will still be there.

MAKES 1 CUP

¾ cup dashi broth

¼ cup soy sauce

2 tablespoons mirin

½ cup dried bonito flakes

Dipping Sauce for Cold Soba

It's not just soy sauce and much better than the stuff you find in fancy food stores. And it works for other cold noodles too.

1. Combine the dashi, soy sauce, and mirin in a saucepan and bring to a boil.

2. Remove the pot from the heat and add the bonito flakes. Stir until they're saturated and then let the pot stand until it reaches room temperature.

3. Strain out the flakes.

Serve at room temperature with soba or any other cold Japanese noodles. A proper serving of cold soba includes the noodles (page 94), the dipping sauce, ¼ cup grated daikon, a teaspoon of wasabi (the Japanese green horseradish sauce) on the side, and some finely chopped scallion and nori sprinkled on top.

Simple Japanese Noodles in Broth

Is this broth suspiciously similar to the soba dipping sauce on page 96? Well . . . yes, both have all the basic Japanese flavors in a pot.

1. Combine the dashi, soy sauce, and mirin in large pot and bring to a boil. Add the bonito flakes, give the mixture a stir, and remove from the heat.

2. Let the flakes steep in the mixture about 30 minutes. Then strain the flakes out. If the flakes are boiled—or even simmered too long—the broth will become bitter.

3. Return the broth to medium heat and simmer until it's hot, about 10 minutes.

4. Put the cooked noodles in serving bowls and ladle the broth over the noodles. Use a fork to stir and make sure the noodles don't clump up.

Sprinkle the scallion greens and nori on top and serve right away.

5 cups dashi broth

½ cup soy sauce

½ cup mirin

1 cup dried bonito flakes

8 ounces soba noodles, cooked, rinsed, and drained (recipe page 94)*

½ cup chopped scallion greens

¼ cup nori, cut into matchstick-sized strips

*Udon noodles are also fine here.

GOD MUST LOVE INSTANT RAMEN

About 95 billion packs of instant ramen are consumed around the world every year; that's about 316 packs for every American—although we're only responsible for about 5 percent of those, according to the World Instant Noodles Association. Even though they're a modern processed food product, instant ramen dominates the world of noodles. To paraphrase Abraham Lincoln, God must love instant noodles, because he made them in so many varieties. Those little rectangular packs might just be the world's most widely consumed noodle form.

I came up with a two-phase plan for greater instant ramen understanding. First, I would visit ethnic grocery markets representing all of Asia and create my own collection. I would then taste them all. It seemed like a good idea at the time; I imagined myself with dozens of varieties, trying to gain understanding of the flavors behind each food culture. My remarks would be witty and insightful, shedding new light on how the world's foods intersect.

Being out on the road changed everything; after I'd seen fifty or sixty different instant ramen packs, they all started to look the same. At the ultra-Japanese Mitsuwa Marketplace, the flavors resembled those offered in local, artisan, fresh ramen shops with varieties like miso and soy sauce.At Super H Mart, the Korean mega-grocery, noodle packs displayed that distinctive Korean script and flavors like *bibim raymon* and curry along with the familiar flavors of beef and seafood. The biggest surprise was Phil-Am, the Philippine grocery, which had so much instant ramen that it was in a separate section, away from the other noodles, indicating to me that they were considered a different food altogether.

A few more shops and I was back home. I realized that even though I had an astounding array of varieties sitting in my kitchen, there was no way I could taste them all. I needed to try at least a few, though. I started with Shio Ramen Japanese Style Noodles. *Shio* seemed like a flavor that could have some pretense of authentic Japaneseness, but it was the taste and color of the cheapest chicken bouillion cubes imaginable. Sadly, during one time or another in my life, I'd eaten thousands of packs of instant noodles that tasted just like this.

Next up was Lucky Me! brand Pancit Canton from the Philippines. I chose it because I didn't want another bowl of bouillon cube, and the words EXTRA HOT CHILE FLAVOR in flaming red letters encouraged me. Indeed, upon opening it, there were little plastic packets of soy sauce and hot mustard as a sort of reference to overseas Cantonese food. Unlike all the others, the Lucky Me! product required mixing the several seasoning packets together to form a paste. I was to then cover the paste with boiled, strained noodles. I did as I was told and wound up with something salty, spicy, and, under the right circumstances, delicious. This got me excited enough to want to try even more.

Since spice seemed to help things along, the next one I tasted was Wai Wai brand sour soup flavor from Thailand. Inside, it had a packet of thick sludge that looked like curry paste, and as I examined it, I was really curious to taste it. That packet of paste tasted exactly like the jars of instant Tom Yum soup base that show up in all sorts of Asian grocery stores. It wasn't bad though.

Over the next couple of days, I tasted more varieties and soon realized they were all pretty similar. The flavors of salt, MSG (another salt, actually), sesame oil, and chile wore on me. Instant ramen always struck me as useful; you could take it camping and have something warm that required very little fuel to cook. Or packs could be distributed to people in a crisis, needing only a small amount of boiling water to make a meal. If there was a choice between instant ramen and typical fast food, I'd choose instant ramen at least part of the time.

Under any other circumstances, though, I think I'd go for something else. Spaghetti with a bit of butter and cheese, and Poor Man's Pasta (page 51) aren't that much more complicated to prepare and are far more gratifying to eat.

ITALY

Basic Tomato Sauce

They don't call this basic for nothing. With a bit of it and some pasta, you have a meal.

1. Heat the oil in a heavy skillet over medium heat, add the oregano, thyme, pepper, and garlic, and cook, stirring, until the garlic turns translucent, about 4 minutes.

2. Lower the heat to medium-low. Add the tomato and simmer, stirring occasionally, until the flavors combine and approximately one-quarter of the liquid evaporates, about 15 minutes.

3. Taste the sauce and see if it needs salt; add it if it does. Because canned tomatoes differ so much, you have to taste and test. Serve warm over pasta, or use in other recipes as called for.

MAKES 3 CUPS

1 tablespoon olive oil

2 teaspoons dried oregano

1 teaspoon dried thyme

½ teaspoon freshly ground pepper

2 cloves garlic, crushed and chopped

3 cups canned crushed tomato

½ teaspoon salt (optional)

MAKES 2 SERVINGS

Orecchiette with Turnip Greens:
Orecchiette con Cime di Rapa

4 cups fresh turnip greens
with the stems removed*

1 tablespoon salt + 1 teaspoon salt

¼ cup olive oil

4 anchovy fillets packed in olive oil

1 tablespoon chopped
fresh hot pepper

5 cloves fresh garlic, peeled
and sliced in half

8 ounces dry orecchiette pasta

2 tablespoons freshly
grated Parmesan cheese

*Substitute 2 cups of chopped
frozen turnip greens if you must. In
that case, skip step 1 and add the
defrosted greens at step 4.

Watch the movement from
pot to pot carefully!

Back in the days when I thought Italian cuisine was something you could only get in restaurants, I had no idea that turnips were part of it. In fact, Italians eat a far wider range of foods than any Italian American restaurant menu would ever let on. And in case you're wondering, *orecchiette* means "little ears" in Italian. An almost identical Chinese pasta shape is called cat's ears in English.

1. Bring 4 quarts of water to a boil in a large pot and add the turnip greens and tablespoon of salt. Reduce the heat to medium and simmer until the leaves are tender, about 4 minutes. Remove the turnip greens from the pot and reserve the salted water for cooking the pasta. Drain the turnip greens and set them aside.

2. Put a large skillet on medium-low heat and add the oil and anchovies. Cook and stir until the anchovies have completely broken up and dissolved in the oil, about 3 minutes.

3. Increase the heat to medium and mix in the hot pepper and garlic and cook, stirring frequently, until the garlic begins to brown at the edges and the peppers are tender, about 10 minutes.

4. Mix in the cooked turnip greens and teaspoon of salt and cook, stirring occasionally, until they've absorbed the anchovy/oil mixture, about 10 minutes.

5. While the turnip greens are cooking, put the reserved salted water back on high heat and cook the orecchiette for the time indicated on the package. Then drain the pasta and add it to the pan with the greens.

Toss until the pasta and greens are evenly distributed and serve right away with plenty of grated Parmesan cheese.

Pasta with Capers, Anchovies, and Tomatoes:
Pasta alla Puttanesca
〜

You might know what the name means, but how many of you can make the dish from scratch? Historians say that it was first called "Whore-Style Sauce" in the 1950s. These ingredients come up so frequently—and are so strongly associated with Southern Italian cooking—I suspect that what was invented was the name, not the flavors.

What's behind the name, you ask? My theory is that you have to be a pretty tough character to cook up all these strong flavors in one dish.

1. Put the oil, oregano, chile flakes, and black pepper in a large skillet over medium-low heat, and cook and stir until all the ingredients are coated with the oil, about 1 minute.

2. Mix in the anchovies and cook and stir until they dissolve into the oil, about 3 minutes. You may have to crush them a bit with a wooden spoon to get them to dissolve.

3. Mix in the garlic, olives, and capers and cook, stirring frequently, until the garlic begins to brown at the edges, about 5 minutes.

4. Mix in the tomato. Cook with occasional stirring until about a quarter of the liquid has evaporated and the raw tomato taste is gone, about 20 minutes.

MAKES 4 SERVINGS

3 tablespoons olive oil

2 teaspoons dried oregano

1 tablespoon crushed dried red chile pepper

1 teaspoon freshly ground black pepper

6 anchovy fillets packed in olive oil

3 tablespoons crushed and chopped fresh garlic

¼ cup chopped black olives

2 tablespoons capers, rinsed and drained

3 cups canned crushed tomato

1 pound spaghetti, *bucatini*, or linguine, cooked and drained

5. Toss with the pasta and serve.

Note: Don't even think about adding extra salt to this sauce—the anchovies, capers, and olives will bring plenty!

THE TWIRL

A SIMPLE QUESTION: is the act of twirling spaghetti on a fork, aided by a soup spoon, authentically Italian? I typed it into a well-known search engine and was offered a $10 battery-powered fork. I didn't have to order one to imagine the many things that could go wrong: If the switch stuck in the on position, I could splatter red sauce all over the dining room. If the batteries ran out while twirling especially long and unruly strands of pasta, I would have to resort to cutting them with a knife—something I already knew was in bad taste.

As an outsider, the idea of an electric gadget at the Italian dining table seemed wrong. I couldn't imagine my fussy Italian wife and her even more fussy relatives with a battery-powered fork, but they do use a rechargeable electric cheese grater, equally absurd in my eyes—yet perfectly acceptable to them.

Still, though—the custom had to come from somewhere, and Italian customs almost always have Italian roots, no matter how far from the source they've traveled in the meantime. That same search directed me to an article in the *New York Times* by food writer Craig Claiborne published in 1982. Not many of us remember that year too well, at least when it comes to Italian restaurants, so I'll fill you in. This was the beginning of the end of French rule in the fine dining world. Italian chefs were still trying to convince us that their restaurants could be fancy and formal. (I know . . .

telling this to today's culinary students is like telling them about the days before refrigeration . . . but that's the way it was.)

The thrust of the *Times* article, like so much written about Italian cooking in those days, was that Italian cuisine was too refined for such silly things as spaghetti twirling. It only briefly mentioned the obvious: If you cooked spaghetti the way most Italians liked it, it would be too stiff to twirl on a fork. When it's cooked al dente, it will just fall off the fork if you try the twirl. I recalled the spaghetti I'd eaten in any number of Italian hostel and mountain hut dining rooms (places Craig Claiborne never set foot in, trust me). Any attempt at twirling that spaghetti on a fork would have given you an eyeful of red sauce. Around Rome, pasta cooked for the locals almost had crunch.

How was it that I didn't pick up on this? Was there some obscure place in Italy where pasta was cooked longer and people twirled it on their forks? Maybe. Back in Italy, people ate pasta that was only slightly more tender than pretzel sticks and viewed spaghetti that was cooked enough to twirl on a fork as suitable only for those with advanced oral diseases.

Americans take their pasta soft and their vegetables crunchy. Italians go the other way—spaghetti with crunch, and broccoli so soft, you could cut the stems with a spoon.

If *al dente* is Italian, than the spoon twirl must be American.

MAKES 4 SERVINGS

Buckwheat Pasta with Cabbage, Potatoes, and Cheese: *Pizzoccheri della Valtellina*

1 cup buckwheat flour

1 cup durum semolina flour + semolina flour for kneading

1 teaspoon salt + 1 tablespoon for the boiling water

1 cup warm water for the dough

2 cups diced Yukon Gold or other yellow potato

2 cups sliced savoy cabbage

1 cup diced fontina cheese*

¼ cup freshly grated Parmesan cheese

¼ cup unsalted butter

1 teaspoon freshly ground pepper

3 fresh sage leaves

*No, the Alpine shepherds of Lombardia didn't use fontina. They would have chosen *Valtellina Casera,* a very similar, but almost impossible to find (unless you're in Valtellina, of course), regional cheese. If you can get it, use it; otherwise, go with fontina, which you can usually find at supermarket cheese counters.

In the far north of Italy, where the climate is brutal and the land more suited for grazing than farming, buckwheat is the pasta flour of choice, and *pizzoccheri*, a flat ribbon pasta, has been a staple. There, cheese goes with everything. The Graubünden region of Switzerland also claims this dish as a local specialty, but with a name as Italian as *pizzoccheri*, we'll keep it here, in the Italian section. People eat it with joy, in both places.

Although it is sometimes possible to find premade *pizzocccheri* in American specialty stores, in this recipe, we make them from scratch. Substitute store-bought if you like.

1. Combine the buckwheat flour, semolina flour, and the teaspoon of salt in a large bowl and add the cup of warm water. Mix—first with a wooden spoon, then with your hands—until a dough forms. If the mixture remains crumbly, add water, 1 tablespoon at a time, until it's soft enough to knead. If the mixture is too soft and sticky, add semolina flour, 1 tablespoon at a time, until a dough forms.

2. Sprinkle semolina flour on a flat surface and knead the dough on it until it's pliable enough to run through a pasta machine, about 8 minutes. Then let the dough rest for 20 minutes.

3. Run the dough through a pasta machine until you have flat sheets. On my machine, I go for number 3, a fairly thick setting. It takes 10 or 15 passes through thicker settings to reach this point. Sprinkle the dough sheets with a bit more semolina and let them dry flat for at least 60 minutes.

4. Cut the dough into strips ½-inch wide and dry them flat or on a pasta rack for at least 60 minutes more. (At this point, if you let the noodles dry completely, they can be stored in an airtight container for at least three months.)

5. Bring 6 quarts of water to a boil in a large pot and add the salt and potatoes. Reduce the heat to medium and cook, stirring occasionally, until the potatoes are tender, about 5 minutes.

6. Mix in the cabbage and *pizzoccheri* and cook, stirring occasionally, until it's tender, about 5 minutes.

7. Drain the pasta and vegetables, put in a large bowl, and immediately mix in the fontina, Parmesan, butter, pepper, and sage leaves. Toss until the heat of the pasta melts the cheeses and butter. If you move quickly enough, the pasta will be evenly coated.

Serve right away. It's delicious warm, but a congealed mess afterwards.

Spaghetti with Cured Pork and Eggs:
Spaghetti alla Carbonara

Italy's second-most-famous tomatoless recipe after pesto sauce (page 117), *Spaghetti alla Carbonara* earned its fame with the inclusion of *guanciale*, a hard-to-find—although easily substituted—ingredient. As for the name, *carbonara* is a reference to charcoal makers; could this be what they ate when they were off in the forest tending to their kilns? Maybe, but the main ingredients, bacon and eggs—and *guanciale* is very much an Italian form of bacon—strongly resembles food shipments sent by the United States after World War II.

MAKES 4 SERVINGS

2 tablespoons olive oil

2 cups chopped *guanciale*, pancetta, or Canadian bacon

½ cup grated pecorino Romano cheese

1 teaspoon freshly ground pepper

2 eggs, beaten

1 pound spaghetti, cooked and drained (time it carefully, it has to be very hot when the ingredients are combined)

One more thing: There's one really important ingredient in this dish—timing. If you bring the spaghetti and eggs together when the pasta is very hot, it works. If you wait, you have raw egg soup.

1. Put the oil and meat in a skillet over high heat and cook and stir until the meat begins to brown at the edges, about 5 minutes. Remove from the heat and set aside.

2. Combine the cheese, pepper, and eggs in a large bowl and stir to make sure all the ingredients are well-distributed.

3. Add the cooked, hot spaghetti to the bowl of egg/cheese mixture and toss until the egg has been cooked by the heat of the spaghetti, about 2 minutes. Then add the cooked meat and make sure that it too is evenly mixed into the pasta.

Serve right away with a bit more grated cheese.

Pasta with Pork and Saffron: *Strozzapreti alla Pastora*

MAKES 4 SERVINGS

If you have a modest command of Italian, the word *strozzapreti* may give you pause: "priest stranglers." At least one Italian priest ate too many too fast, thereby earning this pasta its somewhat frightening name. If the image of choking clergymen isn't for you, substitute cavatelli.

1. Put a large skillet over medium heat and add the oil and onion. Cook, stirring frequently, until the onion is translucent, very tender, and starting to brown at the edges, about 20 minutes.

2 tablespoons olive oil

2 cups sliced onion

8 ounces mild Italian pork sausage meat

1 cup dry red wine

2 cups chicken broth

¼ cup heavy cream

1 cup ricotta cheese

½ teaspoon saffron threads

1 teaspoon salt (optional)

1 teaspoon freshly ground pepper

1 pound *strozzapreti* or cavatelli pasta, cooked and drained

2 tablespoons shredded pecorino Romano cheese

2. Mix in the sausage meat and cook, continuing to stir frequently, until the meat is browned, about 15 minutes. Use the back of a wooden spoon to break the meat up into smaller pieces while it's cooking.

3. Add the wine and broth and simmer uncovered, stirring occasionally, until the liquid has reduced by half, about 30 minutes.

4. Reduce the heat to medium-low and mix in the cream, ricotta, and saffron and cook, stirring frequently, until all the ingredients have combined, about 15 minutes.

5. Taste the sauce. If it needs salt, add it, then add the pepper. Stir a few times to get everything mixed evenly.

6. To assemble the dish, add the cooked pasta to the pot of sauce, toss until the pasta is well coated, and top with the pecorino Romano cheese.

Macaroni and Bean Soup: *Pasta e Fagoli*

As a boy, I was aware of something called "pasta fazool." I never saw it on a restaurant menu and wasn't offered it at anybody's house. It turns out that this is a misrendering of an old Italian classic, *pasta e fagoli* or, in English, pasta and beans. As it turns out, soups with pasta and beans are made all over Italy; indeed, all over Europe. This one is classic Italian.

1. Put the beans in an uncovered pot with 2 quarts of water over high heat. Bring it to a boil and let boil for 2 minutes. Reduce the heat to medium-low and let the beans simmer, stirring occasionally, until they're tender, about 90 minutes. Rinse, drain, and set aside.

2. Put the olive oil in a heavy pot over medium heat and mix in the anchovies. Stir continuously until the anchovies are dissolved, about 2 minutes.

MAKES 4 SERVINGS

1 cup dried *borlotti* (Roman or cranberry) beans

2 tablespoons olive oil

3 anchovy fillets packed in olive oil

1 teaspoon dried rosemary

1 teaspoon dried thyme

1 teaspoon dried oregano

2 bay leaves

1 cup chopped cooked ham

3 tablespoons fresh garlic, crushed and chopped

2 cups chopped onion

1 cup chopped celery

1 cup chopped carrot

6 cups beef broth

8 ounces *ditalini* or macaroni pasta, cooked and drained

1 teaspoon salt, or to taste

3. Mix in the rosemary, thyme, oregano, and bay leaves and cook, stirring continuously, until all the spices are coated with oil, about 2 minutes.

4. Mix in the ham and cook, stirring occasionally, until the ham begins to brown, about 5 minutes.

5. Mix in the garlic, onion, celery, and carrot and cook, continuing to stir occasionally until the onion begins to brown at the edges, about 30 minutes.

6. Add the broth and cooked beans and simmer, stirring occasionally, until the onions are very tender and translucent, about 60 minutes.

7. Mix in the *ditalini*, give the whole thing 1 minute for the flavors to combine, and taste it. If it needs salt, mix in the 1 teaspoon and taste again. If it needs more, add salt ½ teaspoon at a time until it tastes right. Remember, you can add salt, but you can't remove it.

Serve right away.

Spaghetti with Pesto Sauce: *Spaghetti al Pesto*

Pesto is one of those recipes that's been modified and adapted so often that we forget what's supposed to be in it. Purists will tell you that only certain varieties of basil grown in Liguria can be used; others insist that cilantro is an acceptable substitute. This recipe will give you the real thing, with ingredients you can buy in an American supermarket.

1 cup extra virgin olive oil

2 cups tightly packed fresh basil leaves (make sure the thick stems are discarded)

⅓ cup grated Parmesan cheese

3 cloves fresh garlic

1 tablespoon pine nuts (pignoli)

1. Combine the olive oil, basil, Parmesan, garlic, pine nuts, teaspoon of salt, and pepper in a blender or food processor and pulse until the ingredients combine into a thick, bright green paste, about two minutes. Set aside. This sauce can be prepared in advance and refrigerated or even frozen until needed.

1 teaspoon salt + 1 tablespoon salt for the pasta and vegetable cooking water

1 teaspoon freshly ground pepper

1 cup peeled and diced red potato

1 pound spaghetti or *trenette,* dry

1 cup string beans, cut into thumb-sized lengths

2. Bring 12 cups of water to a boil with the tablespoon of salt in a large pot and mix in the potatoes. Reduce the heat to medium and cook, stirring occasionally, until the potatoes become tender, about 15 minutes.

3. Increase the heat to high and add the spaghetti. Stir until all the pasta is wet. Reduce the heat to medium, mix in the string beans, and cook, stirring occasionally, until the pasta is tender, about 10 minutes. Drain and toss to make sure the potatoes and string beans are evenly distributed in the pasta.

To serve, toss the cooked pasta/potato/string bean mixture with the pesto sauce while the pasta is still hot. Serve right away. True Italophiles will want a bit more Parmesan cheese to sprinkle on top.

Italian Spaghetti with Meat Sauce: *Spaghetti Bolognese*

No Italian pasta dish is more popular than spaghetti and meat sauce. I've had sauces made with lamb, beef, and beans, some that were mild enough for a baby and others that were spicy enough for a chilehead. Few of us here in the States have had the traditional Bolognese sauce—perhaps the mother of all sauces—so here it is, the official recipe as codified in Bologna, Italy, on October 17, 1982. The only changes are those that happened during the conversion from metric to English measurements. Here are all the things that Americans would never put in meat sauce that Italians insist belong there: milk, carrots, butter, bacon, and wine. It's not something you would find at a school lunch.

1. Put the butter and oil in a large skillet over medium heat.

2. When the butter has melted, mix in the carrot, onion, and celery and cook, stirring frequently, until the onion is translucent and browning at the edges, about 15 minutes.

3. Mix in the ground beef, pork, and pancetta, continuing to stir frequently until the meat has browned, about 30 minutes. Use the back of a wooden spoon to break the meat into smaller pieces as it cooks.

4. Reduce the heat to medium-low and mix in the broth, tomato paste, milk, and wine and stir frequently until the liquid evaporates by half, about 40 minutes.

MAKES 4 SERVINGS

2 tablespoons butter

3 tablespoons olive oil

½ cup chopped carrot

1 cup chopped onion

½ cup chopped celery stalk

½ pound ground beef

½ pound ground pork

1 cup chopped pancetta (Italian bacon)

1 cup pork or beef broth

2 tablespoons tomato paste

1 cup whole milk

1 cup red wine

1 teaspoon salt (optional)

1 teaspoon freshly ground black pepper

1 pound spaghetti or other pasta, cooked and drained

¼ cup freshly grated Parmesan cheese

5. Taste the sauce. If it needs it, add the salt, and then mix in the pepper.

6. Serve over spaghetti or other pasta and top with grated cheese.

Note: This is as authentic a recipe as is possible given the acts of translation and measurement conversion. However, if you really want your sauce to taste more Italian and you are buying your groceries here, use a full pound of ground pork instead of the mixture of beef and pork. The change compensates for differences in the flavor of ground beef sold in Italy and the United States.

A TABLE OF WHAT PASTA SHAPE GOES WITH WHICH SAUCE AND WHY I DIDN'T DO ONE

MOST BOOKS ON NOODLES AND PASTA offer some section or chart that lists different shapes and the sauces that go with them. This isn't a bad idea, it's just that this sort of thing can make you feel bound by rules that don't really exist. Instead, I'd like to offer real-time advice on what actual people can do.

Yes, your first choice should be a recipe from this book. However, all of us wind up in a kitchen with a box of pasta and not much more at one time or another and it doesn't hurt to know that there's something you can do.

If you have an Italian-style pasta of practically any shape (flat lasagna sheets not the best choice here) you can simply cook and drain it and then toss with butter and grated Parmesan cheese; 1 tablespoon of each per person. You can also substitute olive oil for the butter when there are concerns about cholesterol. In either case, sprinkle each portion with a bit of salt and pepper too.

With dry pasta and olive oil in the pantry and some butter and cheese in the fridge, there will always be at least part of a meal ready and waiting. Is there a little bit more you can add to make it complete? Take a look at Poor Man's Pasta (recipe page 51). Quick enough and much better than pizza delivery or fast food. Right?

MAKES 4 SERVINGS

1 cup olive oil + 2 tablespoons
for the tomato sauce

4 cups peeled and sliced
Italian eggplant*

1 teaspoon salt

2 teaspoons dried oregano

1 teaspoon dried thyme

1 teaspoon dried rosemary

2 tablespoons crushed
and chopped fresh garlic

3 cups canned crushed tomatoes

4 basil leaves, torn into small pieces

1 pound *bucatini* or other large
pasta shape, cooked and drained

¼ cup shredded ricotta salata or
grated pecorino Romano cheese

Pasta with Eggplant: *Pasta alla Norma*

If you find yourself seeking out the perfect, authentic vegetarian Italian pasta dish, seek no more. *Pasta alla Norma*, with its tomato, eggplant, and dried herbs will be it. And the name? *Norma* is an opera by Vincenzo Bellini, a Sicilian icon. A great way to name this very iconic Sicilian dish.

1. Put the cup of olive oil in a skillet over high heat. The oil temperature should read at least 325 degrees and no more than 375 degrees. With a long-handled spatula or tongs, fry the eggplant until it's well-browned on both sides. When all the eggplant slices are browned, set them aside.

2. Put the 2 tablespoons of oil in a skillet over medium heat and mix in the salt, oregano, thyme, and rosemary and cook, stirring, until all the spices are coated with the oil and you can smell them cooking, about 3 minutes.

3. Add the garlic and cook, stirring frequently, until tender, about 5 minutes.

4. Reduce the heat to medium-low, mix in the tomato and basil and cook, stirring occasionally, until the raw taste is gone and the flavors have combined, about 15 minutes.

5. Assemble the dish by first putting the cooked pasta on a serving platter, then cover the pasta with the browned eggplant strips. Cover that with the tomato sauce, and finally sprinkle with the grated cheese.

*There's plenty of disagreement about how to do this. I prefer slices ¼-inch thick, which are then cut into sticks ¼-inch wide. Dry the eggplant slices with paper towels before frying. If the eggplant isn't dry, it will splatter when placed in the heated oil and give you nasty burns. Also: don't skip this dish just because you can't find Italian eggplant—any type will work.

Ligurian Macaroni, Sausage, and Tripe: *Maccheroni con la Trippa*

MAKES 4 SERVINGS

How far back do traditions go? This dish is made with ingredients that seem to be out of not only another place, but another time. *Maccheroni?* Tripe? A real pot of ancient food. However, as alien as it is, it announces its heritage loud and clear. A real Italian dish to eat on a real Ligurian winter night.

1 tablespoon coarse salt

1½ pounds honeycomb tripe cut into 1 x 3-inch strips

2 tablespoons olive oil

1 teaspoon dried sage

1 pound mild Italian sausage cut into 1-inch pieces

2 tablespoons crushed and chopped fresh garlic

2 cups chopped onion

1 cup chopped celery

1 cup chopped carrot

1 cup canned crushed tomato

1 cup white wine

1 teaspoon salt

1 teaspoon freshly ground pepper

1 cup water

1 pound *maccheroni,* cooked and drained*

2 tablespoons chopped parsley

*Note that this is the Italian shape *maccheroni,* not the American elbows.

1. Bring 3 quarts of water to a boil in a large covered pot and add the coarse salt and tripe. Reduce the heat to medium-low and simmer, stirring occasionally, until the tripe is tender, about 60 minutes. Drain and set aside.

2. Put the oil in a large pot over medium-high heat, mix in the sage and sausage, and cook and stir until the sausage has browned, about 15 minutes.

3. Reduce the heat to medium-low. Mix in the garlic, onion, celery, and carrot and cook, stirring frequently, until the onion is very tender, about 30 minutes.

4. Add the cooked tripe, crushed tomato, wine, salt, pepper, and 1 cup of water. Simmer, uncovered, stirring occasionally, until the flavors have combined and the onions seem ready to dissolve, about 20 minutes.

5. Mix in the cooked *maccheroni* and chopped parsley and give it a few stirs. Serve right away with plenty of grated Parmesan cheese.

MAKES 4 SERVINGS

⅓ cup extra virgin olive oil

2 tablespoons grated bottarga (dried mullet roe)

1 pound dried angel hair pasta, cooked and drained

Pasta with Bottarga

Bottarga is one of those Italian miracle ingredients. They take the roe from mullet, a cheap and plentiful fish, and dry it in the sun to concentrate its flavors. Then, all you need to do is put a bit of it on cooked pasta and watch the flavors explode.

1. Combine the olive oil and bottarga together in a serving bowl large enough to hold the cooked pasta. You'll need to mix them a bit to combine them.

2. Combine the cooked pasta with the oil and bottarga mixture. Toss until all the pasta is coated with the oil and the bottarga is evenly distributed.

Serve right away.

PART III
A WORLD OF NOODLES

KOREA

KOREAN NOODLES 101

In Italy, you can walk down a supermarket aisle and see pasta in an astounding array of shapes, from arm-long tubes to rice-like grains. Yet—unless you've stumbled into the gluten-free section—every one of them is made at least partially from wheat. There's a bit more variety in China, where rice noodles are pretty well represented too. If you want to stray from wheat and rice though, your best bet is to head over to Korea.

You won't have much trouble finding wheat and rice noodles in Korean markets. You'll also find noodles made from a wide variety of unique—or at least unique to noodles—ingredients like kudzu, sweet potato starch, acorn flour, corn flour, pumpkin, and potato starch.

Besides *japchae* (page 131), *jajang myun* (page 132), *jjamppong* (page 134), and *bibim guksu* (page 136), there are a whole host of Korean noodle dishes and types worth exploring. *Naeng myeon* are buckwheat noodles that are served ice-cold. There are restaurants that carry this to an extreme and put ice cubes in the broth itself. *Cheonsachae*, made from seaweed jelly, and *dotori guksu*—made from acorns—look a bit like whole wheat spaghetti, and like so many others mentioned here, find their way into cold soups and salads.

Not long ago, I sat down to a bowl of *bibim naeng myeon* at a local Korean noodle restaurant. On the menu, they were just called noodles, but when I started eating, I realized that I was in a whole different ballgame. Presented cold under chile paste and vegetables, the *naeng myeon* somehow managed to be chewy and slippery at the same time. As if the dish wasn't startling enough, the server darted back with yellow plastic squeeze bottles of hot mustard and vinegar. I poured it on and he nodded with approval.

After I ate, I strolled over to a nearby Korean grocery and checked out the noodle aisle. There were bags marked "Chinese Noodle" that looked like bundles of fiber optics and had sweet potato starch as their only listed ingredient, and others that appeared to be packages of edible grilling skewers. Few were mentioned in either English-language Korean cookbooks or on neighborhood restaurant menus. I left knowing one thing—whatever it was that Korean chefs did with these noodles, there'd be the bite of chile, the zing of vinegar, and a texture I'd never encountered before.

Fried Cellophane Noodles: *Japchae*

No country pushes the boundaries of the world of noodles like Korea. There, noodles of rice and wheat are common, and so are ones made from bean or acorn flour. *Japchae*, the popular Korean fried noodle dish, uses noodles made from sweet potato starch.

1. Cut soaked noodles into 6-inch-long pieces and set aside.

2. Mix the soy sauce, rice wine, sugar, and water together in a bowl. Make sure that the sugar is dissolved before you proceed.

3. Put the chicken strips in the soy mixture and let marinate in the refrigerator for at least 30 minutes.

4. Put the oil in a large wok or large skillet over high heat. When it's hot, mix in the garlic, onion, carrot, mushroom, and bell pepper and cook, stirring, until the onion is tender, about 10 minutes.

5. Mix in the chicken and half the marinating liquid and cook and stir until the meat appears cooked, about 5 minutes.

6. Add the soaked noodles and spinach and cook, stirring, until the noodles have absorbed the liquid that's formed at the bottom of the pan and all the ingredients are evenly distributed, about 3 minutes.

7. Sprinkle the sesame seeds on top and serve right away.

1 package (12 ounces) Korean sweet potato noodles (*dang myun*), soaked, rinsed, and drained

½ cup soy sauce

2 tablespoons rice wine

¼ cup sugar

½ cup water

1 pound boneless chicken thighs or breasts, cut in ½ -inch strips

2 tablespoons peanut oil

2 tablespoons crushed and chopped garlic

1 cup sliced onion

½ cup shredded carrot

1 cup fresh shiitake mushroom cap slices

1 cup red bell pepper strips

1 cup blanched and chopped spinach

2 tablespoons sesame seeds

Noodles with Black Bean Sauce: *Jajang Myun*

MAKES 4 SERVINGS

2 tablespoons peanut oil

¼ cup Korean roasted black bean paste

½ pound boneless pork loin cut into ½-inch cubes

1 tablespoon sugar

1 cup coarsely chopped onion

1 cup peeled potato cut into ½-inch cubes

2 tablespoons crushed and chopped garlic

1 cup coarsely chopped napa cabbage

1 cup zucchini cut into ½-inch cubes

1 pound *somen* (Korean wheat flour noodles), cooked and drained

2 tablespoons sesame oil

This dish started life in the Shandong region of China, where it was called "fried sauce noodles." Then it jumped across to Korea, where Chinese migrants started cooking it. Since then, it's achieved near-national-dish status. In fact, its one hundredth anniversary in Korea was celebrated in 2005.

1. Put the oil and black bean paste in a large skillet or wok over medium heat and stir until the oil and sauce are combined, about 3 minutes.

2. Mix in the pork, sugar, onion, potato, and garlic and cook, stirring frequently, until the potato starts to becomes tender, about 15 minutes.

3. Mix in the cabbage and zucchini and continue to cook, stirring frequently, until the zucchini is tender, about 15 minutes.

4. To serve, ladle the hot sauce over a bed of cooked noodles and then pour a bit of the sesame oil over it.

MAKES 2 SERVINGS

3 tablespoons peanut oil

2 tablespoons Korean red
pepper powder (*gochugaru*)

8 ounces boneless chicken
thigh meat cut into strips

3 tablespoons crushed
and chopped garlic

Spicy Noodle Soup: *Jjamppong*

Jjamppong is a tough dish to pin a nationality on. Its got a Korean name, a Chinese heritage, and some serious claims to popularity in Japan. So what is it? A bowl of Chinese noodle soup spiced up for the Korean market. It worked. Not only did Koreans embrace it, they brought it with them when they opened their own restaurants overseas.

(continued on facing page)

1. Put a wok or large skillet on high heat and add the oil, pepper powder, and chicken. Cook, stirring, until the chicken meat becomes opaque, about 3 minutes.

2. Mix in the garlic and ginger and cook and stir until the garlic starts to become tender, about 5 minutes.

3. Mix in the carrot, scallions, mushroom, cabbage, leeks, and onion and cook, stirring frequently, until the onion starts to become tender, about 5 minutes.

4. Mix in the water and soy sauce and bring to a boil. Then reduce the heat to medium-low and let simmer uncovered, stirring occasionally, until the carrots and leeks are tender, about 40 minutes.

5. Mix in the *wakame*, squid rings, shrimp, and sesame seeds. Cook and stir until the shrimp becomes opaque, about 3 minutes. Remove from heat.

6. To assemble the dish, first put a heap of cooked noodles at the bottom of each serving bowl and ladle the chicken/seafood/broth mixture over them. Then garnish with half a hard-cooked egg.

2 tablespoons finely chopped fresh ginger

1 cup thinly sliced or shredded carrot

½ cup scallions cut into 2-inch lengths

1 cup sliced fresh shiitake mushroom caps

1 cup sliced napa cabbage

1 cup leeks cut into 2-inch lengths

1 cup sliced onion

8 cups water

2 tablespoons soy sauce

1 teaspoon wakame (dried seaweed)

8 ounces squid rings

4 ounces peeled and deveined raw shrimp

2 tablespoons sesame seeds

1 pound fresh ramen or lo mein noodles, cooked and drained

1 hard-cooked egg, sliced in half

MAKES 4 SERVINGS

¼ cup Korean chile pepper paste (*gochujang*)

2 teaspoons hot mustard

¼ cup rice wine vinegar

2 tablespoons soy sauce

2 tablespoons Karo syrup*

2 tablespoons sesame oil

2 tablespoons sesame seeds

1 cup thinly sliced napa cabbage

1 cup matchstick-sized carrot slices

1 cup matchstick-sized cucumber slices

1 cup matchstick-sized Asian pear slices

½ cup shredded scallions

1 pound *somen* (Korean wheat flour noodles), cooked, rinsed, and drained

1 cup chopped napa cabbage *kimchi*

2 hard cooked eggs, cut in half

*In Korea, you'd use malt syrup, or *mul yut*.

Cold Noodles with Vegetables: *Bibim Guksu*

Here's Korea's addition to the world of cold noodle salads. This one has plenty of spice, some sweet, and a fistful of vegetables too.

1. Combine the pepper paste, mustard, vinegar, soy sauce, Karo syrup, sesame oil, and sesame seeds in a large bowl and mix well. Refrigerate for at least 1 hour so that the flavors combine.

2. Toss the cabbage, carrot, cucumber, pear, and scallion together and set aside.

3. To assemble the dish, put a quarter of the sauce at the bottom of each serving bowl, then put a serving of the cooked noodles on top of the puddle of sauce. Cover the noodles with the vegetable mixture, spoon some of the *kimchi* over the vegetables, and put half of a cooked egg on top.

Serve right away.

THE PHILIPPINES

Fried Rice Noodles: *Pancit Bihon*

I've always wondered how the foods of Thailand and Japan have become so popular, while dishes from the Philippines remain almost unknown. This recipe, with rice noodles, vegetables, and chicken, makes a good introduction.

1. Put a wok or large skillet on high heat and add the oil, garlic, and onion. Cook and stir until the onion starts to become tender, about 4 minutes.

2. Mix in the carrot, celery, cabbage, and snow peas and cook, stirring regularly, until the cabbage is tender, about 10 minutes.

3. Add the chicken and continue to stir until the chicken is cooked through, about 10 minutes.

4. Push the vegetables to the side of the pan and add the broth, soy sauce, and fish sauce and bring to a boil, about 3 minutes. Then give the pan a few big stirs to combine the liquid and cooked food.

5. Add the noodles and toss in the pan until the liquid is absorbed and the meat and vegetables are well distributed, about 5 minutes. Serve right away.

2 tablespoons peanut oil

3 tablespoons crushed and chopped garlic

1 cup sliced onion

½ cup shredded carrot

1 cup celery sticks

2 cups savoy cabbage, cut into ½-inch-wide strips

1 cup snow peas

1 pound boneless chicken breasts or thighs, cut into ½-inch-wide strips

1 cup chicken broth

1 tablespoon soy sauce

1 teaspoon Thai or Vietnamese fish sauce

8 ounces fine rice noodles, soaked and drained*

*These are called *pancit bihon* at Filipino shops. You can also use Vietnamese or Thai rice noodles.

Spaghetti with Sliced Hot Dogs

MAKES 4 SERVINGS

2 tablespoons peanut oil

2 cups chopped onion

3 tablespoons chopped fresh garlic

1 teaspoon sugar

½ teaspoon salt

½ teaspoon freshly ground pepper

½ pound ground beef

½ pound sliced hot dogs

½ cup whole milk

½ cup ketchup

1 cup canned crushed tomato

1 pound spaghetti, cooked and drained

When foods start traveling, they show up in their destination countries in surprising ways. Neither spaghetti nor hot dogs are native to the Philippines, yet somehow they combine here to become something totally different than the inventor of either would have ever foreseen.

1. Put the oil, onion, and garlic in a heavy pot over medium-low heat and cook and stir until the onion is very tender, about 20 minutes.

2. Mix in the sugar, salt, pepper, ground beef, and hot dog and cook, stirring occasionally, until the beef is well browned, about 20 minutes more.

3. Mix in the milk, ketchup, and crushed tomato and simmer uncovered, stirring occasionally, until the taste of raw tomato is gone and the flavors have combined, about 30 minutes. If the sauce becomes too thick, add water, ¼ cup at a time, until it's the same thickness as a typical pasta sauce.

4. Serve over the spaghetti.

VIETNAM

NOODLES IN THE MORNING

For most of us here in the United States, noodles aren't a morning food. That doesn't mean that nobody eats noodles for breakfast, it's just that we have to poke around a bit to find them. If there's one country that embraces a bowl of steaming noodles in the morning, it's Vietnam, where there's a long history of starting the day with the classic beef noodle soup *pho* (recipe page 145).

I was dubious about this at first. Vietnamese food authority Andrea Nguyen not only assured me that pho was a popular breakfast, she also had fond memories of Sunday after-church meals of pho made by her grandmother. In a tone of near-rapture, she told me to "forget church coffee hour and make pho instead."

She went on to say that in Vietnam "we eat pho really early, before it gets hot—when it's only 85 degrees." This really made me wonder about the relationship between climate and cuisine. Could a steaming bowl of noodle soup be the national dish of one of the hottest, muggiest countries on the planet? Pho is what I would want in Siberia. Andrea felt differently. In fact, pho is the perfect Vietnamese food: a fusion of cuisines in a bowl. The beef is French, the noodles Chinese, and the herbs the taste of Vietnam itself. Climate had nothing to do with it.

I wanted to try a bowl of pho in the morning to find out for myself. Normally, the Asian restaurants in my (very Asian) neighborhood don't start serving until lunch, leaving many people to wonder if these cuisines offer anything for breakfast at all. To my surprise, one local Vietnamese place was already open at 9:30. I headed on over.

On a Saturday morning, I was the only person there. In fact, nobody was manning the front—it was clear that they weren't expecting a customer at that time. Pho may be popular in the morning in Vietnam, but not in New Jersey.

It didn't matter. Within minutes, I had noodle soup in front of me. Despite being described as the "combo bowl," there was nothing but cooked beef. I mixed in the herbs and sprouts and studied for a moment. Before I even tasted, I could see that this was the best bowl in the area; the broth had small bits of beef and a wonderful scent.

Noodles aren't my normal breakfast, and this, as it turns out, is my loss. The soup was gentle. There was none of the thrill (and subsequent stupor) you get from a big plate of eggs and bacon, and yet it had substance. It was more filling than a quick muffin or bagel, too. I wasn't stuffed and didn't want a doughnut an hour later. Andrea had told me, "I hunger for that morning experience, it's extremely soothing and grounding." Even without any childhood memories, I found her comment to hit the nail on the head.

As I was leaving, the owner told me, "In Vietnam, we eat noodle soup in the morning, at lunch, for supper . . . all day! When you wake up, you open your door and a street vendor will bring you your pho, and then, a while later, come back and pick up the empty bowl."

Vietnamese Beef Noodle Soup: *Pho*

A dish must be popular if you can find whole restaurants devoted to it in every corner of the world. Pho, Vietnamese beef noodle soup, meets this criteria with ease. It heads the menu in Paris, Virginia Beach, and Hong Kong too. In its home country, it's everywhere; people begin eating it at the crack of dawn (see sidebar, page 148).

Does the name come from the French *pot-au-feu*? Both dishes require long simmering. Or maybe the Cantonese word for rice noodles, rendered and pronounced as *fun* in English and something a bit closer to *pho* in its native language? Either way, it's the dish that put Vietnamese food on the map.

1. In an oven preheated to 425 degrees, roast the ginger and onion until onion browns at the edges, about 30 minutes. Remove from oven and set aside.

2. Put the oxtail and beef bones in a large pot and add enough water to cover. Bring to a boil over high heat. Let it boil for 1 minute, turn the heat off, remove the oxtail and bones, and discard the water. This step removes impurities and gives a cleaner stock. Don't skip it.

3. Return the oxtail and beef bones to pot and add 5 quarts water. Cook, stirring occasionally, over medium-low heat until the pot comes to a simmer.

(Recipe steps and ingredients list continue on page 146.)

MAKES 4 SERVINGS

1 piece fresh ginger, 3 inches long

2 large onions, peeled and cut in half

2½ pounds oxtail cut into 1- to 2-inch slices

2½ pounds beef soup bones in large chunks

¼ cup Vietnamese or Thai fish sauce

2 tablespoons sugar

10 whole star anise

6 whole cloves

1 cinnamon stick

1 teaspoon fennel seeds

4 bay leaves

Cheesecloth and string for simmering the spices

Chopped cooked beef picked from the bones (optional)

1 tablespoon salt

¼ pound thinly sliced sirloin beef

½ cup thinly sliced red onion

2 tablespoons sliced scallions

2 tablespoons chopped fresh cilantro

2 cups fresh mung bean sprouts

2 tablespoons thinly sliced hot chilies

2 tablespoons fresh Asian basil leaves

2 lime wedges

4 ounces dried fine rice stick noodles, soaked, rinsed, and drained

4. After the liquid simmers for a few minutes, you'll start to see foam and scum form on the surface. This has to be skimmed off. Let the meat simmer covered for 1 hour and skim as necessary. You will probably need to skim 5 or 6 times. Don't forget this step.

5. Mix in the roasted ginger and onions, fish sauce, and sugar and let the pot simmer for 30 more minutes, continuing to skim if necessary.

6. Tie the star anise, cloves, cinnamon stick, fennel, and bay leaves together in a bag made from the cheesecloth and add it to the simmering mixture. Continue cooking, stirring occasionally and skimming as needed, for two more hours. When the broth is cooked, there'll be a combination of strong beef and spice flavors. If you're a fan, you'll recognize it as the flavor of pho when you taste it.

7. After 4 total hours of simmering, strain the liquid and remove the solids. For a more intense flavor, pick the meat off the bones and add the chopped meat back into the broth before discarding the bones. Taste. If the broth is too strong, dilute with water, 1 cup at a time, until it's right. If it's too mild, simmer uncovered over low heat and taste every 20 minutes or so until it's strong enough for your tastes. Let cool. You should have about 12 cups of broth.

If you're making the broth and soup on separate days, stop here. The broth can be stored in the refrigerator for several days. It can also be frozen. Otherwise, it's time to put the dish together.

8. Each serving of soup is individually assembled in the bowl it's eaten out of. If it's not already warm, heat up the broth. You'll need 3 cups per serving.

9. While that's happening, put one quarter of the beef, onion, scallion, and cilantro in each serving bowl along with one quarter of the soaked noodles.

10. Pour the hot broth over the noodle mixture. The heat will quickly cook the beef, onion, scallion, and cilantro.

11. Serve right away with a side dish of sprouts, chiles, basil, and lime wedges. Most serious pho eaters will squeeze the lime over the soup and mix in the sprouts, basil, and chile as they eat.

BONES: THE SKELETON OF SOUP

AT THE TYPICAL VIETNAMESE NOODLE SHOP in the suburban northeastern USA, in my experience, you'll find servers with big smiles offering up bowls of pho with watery broth and dry meat,

and tiny three-dollar cups of coffee. This just isn't right. Classic pho is made from beef broth using bones from real cattle, not from a can or powder. It takes time to get it right. The cooks at shops using instant might be able to sleep later in the morning, but you might wonder how they sleep at night. One of the world's finest noodle soups deserves better.

Pho is the original French/Asian fusion dish. Just remember, it's not pronounced "foe," as in "fee, fi, fo, fum," but "feuwh," as in the French *pot-au-feu*. And while its origins are French, the dish has become something very deeply Asian. Across America, pho restaurants are everywhere; you can order a "big bowl" or an "extra big bowl," and for a bit more, you can add meatballs too. What makes it or breaks it, though, isn't in the bowl, it's in the bones.

Bones make pho a whole different sort of food. The broth I make from beef bones is dark, rich, and mysterious—and the longer I simmer it, the darker it becomes. Lifting a spoonful from the bowl, you can see that it has real body, and tiny flecks of meat. When I add the chopped meat pulled from the simmered bones, the flavor and texture takes another step up. The fragrance of Vietnam infuses the dish—the star anise, cloves, and cinnamon—the bowl in front of you could nourish a nation. Bones give it soul.

It turns out that pho has a sort of rhythm of its own. Really long, followed by short, and ending with quick. In theory, the broth should take about four hours, but in practice, it never seemed like it had cooked long enough. I always finished every cooking session swearing that I'd let the next batch go longer. Afterward, there's the moment or two when you cook the noodles and add the beef, onion, and cilantro. And the finishing touch of sprouts and basil happens at the table, seconds before you eat.

Is instant the devil's dust? Not really. In fact, with the instant and a few basic ingredients, you can make a bowl of pho in less time than it takes most of us to drive to the local Vietnamese restaurant. But when it comes to understanding the cuisine and why so many people are devoted to it, you have to start with bones.

MAKES 4 SERVINGS

¼ cup lime juice

2 tablespoons soy sauce

2 tablespoons Vietnamese
or Thai fish sauce

¼ cup sugar

1 tablespoon chopped fresh
hot red chile pepper

1 tablespoon crushed and
chopped garlic

6 ounces Vietnamese
fine rice noodles

2 cups tender lettuce leaves,
like oak leaf, red leaf, or green
leaf, torn into strips

1 cup mung bean sprouts,
rinsed and drained

½ cup chopped cucumber

½ cup shredded carrot

¼ cup fresh basil leaves

¼ cup fresh mint leaves

¼ cup chopped fresh cilantro

2 cups deep-fried tofu
cut into dice-sized cubes

½ cup chopped peanuts

Vietnamese Noodle Salad: *Bún Chay*

Vietnam's contribution to the world of cold noodles, this dish is perfect for the sort of tropical days that even people from temperate climates experience every now and then.

1. Mix the lime juice, soy sauce, fish sauce, sugar, pepper, and garlic together in a bowl until the sugar dissolves. This may take up to 5 minutes. Let the mixture sit for at least 1 hour for the flavors to combine. If the sugar settles out again, give it a few more stirs.

2. Put the noodles in a heatproof bowl and pour 4 cups of boiling water over them. Allow to stand with occasional stirring until tender, about 10 minutes. Drain and set aside.

3. Toss the lettuce, bean sprouts, cucumber, carrot, basil, mint, and cilantro together in a large bowl. Make sure they're evenly distributed. Set aside.

4. Divide the noodles up into 4 servings and place each on a serving plate. Put a heap of the greens on top of the noodles, set some tofu cubes along the edge, sprinkle with the chopped peanuts, and drizzle with the sauce.

Serve right away. If making ahead, keep all the elements separate until serving time.

MAKES 4 SERVINGS

12 ounces dry fine Asian egg noodles, cooked and drained

2 cups peanut oil + 2 tablespoons for stir-frying

½ cup chicken broth

1 tablespoon oyster sauce

2 tablespoons fish sauce

1 tablespoon soy sauce

1 teaspoon cornstarch

3 tablespoons crushed and chopped fresh garlic

½ cup thinly sliced carrot

1 cup sliced onion

1 pound boneless chicken thighs, cut into strips

2 cups baby bok choy, sliced the long way, into strips

2 cups snow peas

Crispy Fried Egg Noodles: *Mì Xaò Dòn*

Fried noodles actually come in more varieties than the take-out Chinese ones accompanying egg-drop soup. This is Vietnam's crispy version, topped with a stir-fry containing soy sauce and fish sauce—a typical Vietnamese combination.

1. As soon as they're drained and cool enough to touch, form the cooked egg noodles into 4 flat pancakes. Let them sit on sheets of parchment paper until they set and hold together, about 15 minutes.

2. Put the 2 cups of peanut oil in a wok or large skillet over high heat. When the oil reaches 375 degrees—check this with a frying thermometer—use a spatula to carefully place one pancake of noodles in the oil and fry until it's browned, about 3 minutes. Then use a spatula and/or tongs to turn it over and fry the other side, about 1 more minute. Repeat until all the pancakes are fried. Drain them on paper towels and set aside.

3. Combine the chicken broth, oyster sauce, fish sauce, soy sauce, and cornstarch together in a small bowl. Stir until the corn starch is dissolved, about 30 seconds. Set aside.

4. Put the 2 tablespoons of oil in a wok or large skillet over high heat (it's okay to reuse the noodle frying oil) and add the garlic, carrot, and onion. Cook and stir until the onion becomes tender and the garlic browns at the edges, about 3 minutes.

5. Mix in the chicken and cook, stirring, until it's opaque and cooked through, about 3 minutes.

6. Mix in the soy sauce mixture, the bok choy strips, and the snow peas and cook and stir until the snow peas are tender, about 5 minutes.

To assemble the dish, place a fried noodle pancake on a plate and cover with the stir-fry mixture. Serve right away.

MALAYSIA

Fish in a Spicy Tamarind Noodle Soup: *Assam Laksa*

Assam laksa combines the sweet, salty, sour, and hot flavors of Southeast Asia in a single bowl.

1. Combine the shallot, garlic, lemongrass, galangal, ginger, and lime juice in a food processor or blender and purée until you have a smooth paste, about 2 minutes.

2. Bring the 2 quarts of water to a boil in a large pot. When the water is boiling, mix in the blended shallot/garlic mixture, *sambal, belacan,* palm sugar, and laksa leaves. Reduce the heat to medium-low and simmer covered until the flavors have combined and the leaves are very tender, about 30 minutes.

3. Uncover the pot and simmer until about a quarter of the liquid has evaporated, about 30 minutes.

4. Remove from the heat. Let cool for a few minutes and discard the laksa leaves using a skimmer or strainer. Then return the pot to medium-low heat and add the mackerel. Cook with occasional stirring until the mackerel is cooked through, about 15 minutes.

5. Put a quarter of the noodles at the bottom of each serving bowl and ladle the liquid soup over them until they're barely covered. Then garnish with the shallot, pineapple, cucumber, and mint. Serve right away.

1 cup chopped shallot + ¼ cup thinly sliced shallot for garnish

⅓ cup whole garlic cloves

¼ cup chopped lemongrass stalks

2 tablespoons chopped fresh or frozen galangal root

3 tablespoons chopped fresh ginger

½ cup lime juice

2 quarts water

2 tablespoons *sambal* (Malaysian chile paste)

2 teaspoons *belacan* (Malaysian fermented shrimp paste)

¼ cup crushed palm sugar

¼ cup laksa leaves

1 pound Spanish mackerel or mackerel fillet, cut in thin strips

8 ounces thick rice noodles, soaked and drained

½ cup crushed pineapple

½ cup cucumber strips

2 tablespoons fresh mint leaves

MAKES 2 SERVINGS

6 dried red hot chiles

1 teaspoon *sambal* (Malaysian chile paste)

1 tablespoon *belacan* (Malaysian fermented shrimp paste)

½ cup water

2 tablespoons lard

2 tablespoons crushed and chopped fresh garlic

1 tablespoon thick soy sauce

1 tablespoon soy sauce

1 teaspoon ground white pepper

1 teaspoon sugar

½ pound boneless chicken thigh meat cut into thumbnail-sized pieces

2 cups coarsely chopped *choy sum* cabbage or Chinese broccoli

6 ounces wide rice noodles, soaked, rinsed, and drained

1 cup mung bean sprouts, rinsed and drained

¼ cup chopped scallion greens

2 tablespoons sliced fresh red hot chiles

Malaysian Stir-Fried Flat Noodles: *Char Kway Teow*

You can learn a lot about a culture from a plate of fried noodles. *Char kway teow* recounts the story of Malaysian cuisine. There's the yin and yang of the food itself, fresh ingredients mixed with fermented. In this part of the world, you can't have one without the other. Then there's the lard. The dish may be tropical, but it's fuel for hard labor and filled with calories. And finally, the use of rice noodles tells you that it's from a place that's too far south to grow or store wheat. Of course, no matter how much you learn, you don't really know a cuisine without cooking it.

1. Combine the chiles, *sambal, belacan,* and water in a food processor and blend into a paste. Set aside.

2. Put a wok or large skillet on high heat and add the lard and garlic. Stir-fry until the garlic starts to brown, about 1 minute.

3. Mix in the blended chile mixture from step 1, thick soy sauce, soy sauce, white pepper, and sugar and stir-fry until they all combine, about 1 minute.

4. Add the chicken and stir-fry until the meat is coated with the sauce mixture and begins to brown, about 3 minutes.

5. Mix in the cabbage pieces and stir-fry until they're tender and the chicken meat is fully cooked, about 3 minutes.

6. Add the noodles and bean sprouts and use tongs and/or wooden spoons to make sure that all the ingredients are evenly distributed, about 2 minutes.

7. Remove the pan from the heat and toss with the scallions and hot chile slices.

Serve right away.

CAMBODIA

Pork and Rice Noodle Soup: *Ka Tieu*

Ka tieu, Cambodia's national dish, is easy enough to describe—it's similar to Vietnamese pho (page 145), but with pork broth instead of beef broth. For most of us, this means making broth from scratch, so it's time to get some good-sized pork bones and pull out that big stock pot.

1. Put the bones and 5 quarts of water in a large pot over high heat and bring to a boil. Let boil for 30 seconds and remove from the heat. Discard the water and reserve the bones.

2. Put the scalded bones and onion in 5 quarts of fresh water, bring to a boil over high heat, and let it boil for 30 seconds. Then reduce the heat to medium-low and simmer covered, stirring occasionally, until the bones have given up their flavor and the onion has dissolved, about 3 hours. If any scum forms on the surface, skim it off and discard. You should have about 3 quarts of broth at the end.

3. Remove the bones and any remaining bits of onion from the liquid and discard. Add the pork strips and continue to simmer until the meat is barely cooked through, about 30 minutes.

4. While the broth is simmering, heat the oil in a small skillet over medium heat, mix in the garlic, and cook and stir until it browns at the edges, about 5 minutes. Remove the garlic from the oil and set aside, keeping the oil in the skillet.

MAKES 4 SERVINGS

5 pounds pork soup bones (any good Asian butcher will have these)

1 large onion, peeled and cut in quarters

5 quarts water

1 pound boneless pork tenderloin, cut in ½-inch strips

¼ cup peanut oil

¼ cup crushed and chopped fresh garlic

8 ounces ground pork

½ teaspoon salt + 2 teaspoons salt

2 tablespoons sugar

½ pound shelled and deveined shrimp

2 cups mung bean sprouts

8 ounces fine rice noodles, soaked and drained

½ cup chopped scallions

½ cup fresh cilantro leaves

¼ cup sliced, fresh hot red chiles

2 tablespoons soy sauce

5. Put the ground pork and ½ teaspoon of salt in the skillet with the reserved oil and cook over medium heat until the pork browns, about 5 minutes. Use a wooden spoon to break the ground pork into the smallest pieces possible as it cooks. Set it aside.

6. Add the salt, sugar, and shrimp to the broth and cook, stirring, until the shrimp are opaque, about 3 minutes. If you're not ready to serve the dish right away, remove the cooked shrimp and set aside.

7. Assemble the soup by first putting a heap of soaked rice noodles in each serving bowl. Add 2 tablespoons of cooked ground pork and 1 tablespoon of fried garlic, then ladle the hot broth over all, making sure everybody gets both pork strips and shrimp. Garnish with the scallions, cilantro, hot chiles, and soy sauce.

THAILAND

MAKES 2 SERVINGS

1 tablespoon tamarind concentrate

3 tablespoons Thai or
Vietnamese fish sauce

2 tablespoons crushed palm sugar

1 teaspoon dried chile flakes

3 tablespoons peanut oil

½ cup minced shallots

1 tablespoon crushed and
chopped garlic

1 cup pressed tofu cut into
dice-sized cubes

2 eggs

4 ounces fine Thai rice noodles,
soaked, rinsed, and drained

½ pound peeled and
deveined shrimp

½ cup Chinese chives,
cut into 2-inch strips

1 cup mung bean sprouts,
rinsed and drained

1 lime, cut in quarters

Fried Rice Noodles: *Pad Thai*

Are you old enough to remember when this dish was considered exotic? Thai food is a staple of strip malls today and that's led to lots of people thinking that Thailand's national dish is nothing more than a greasy mess. Make it yourself to find out how it's really supposed to taste.

1. Combine the tamarind concentrate, fish sauce, palm sugar, and chile flakes in a bowl and stir until the sugar dissolves. Set aside. (You may have to let it soak a while in order for the sugar to fully dissolve.)

2. Put a wok or large skillet on high heat and add the peanut oil. The hotter you can make your pan, the better the dish will taste. Add the shallots and cook and stir until they start to brown, about 2 minutes.

3. Mix in the garlic and tofu. Cook and stir until everything is well combined, about 2 minutes.

4. Push the cooking ingredients to the side of the pan and add the eggs. Scramble until they start to firm up. Then toss the entire mixture together.

5. Add the soaked and drained noodles and toss until all the ingredients are well combined, about 2 minutes.

6. Add the tamarind sauce and cook, stirring, until the sauce has been completely absorbed, about 2 minutes.

7. Mix in the shrimp, chives, and bean sprouts, and cook and stir until the shrimp turn opaque and all the ingredients are evenly mixed together, about 3 minutes. Serve hot, with lime quarters.

MAKES 2 SERVINGS

3 cups peanut oil + 2
tablespoons for stir-frying

6 ounces fine rice noodles, dry*

3 tablespoons small dried shrimp

½ cup chopped Chinese sausage

2 tablespoons crushed
and chopped fresh garlic

2 tablespoons chopped
fresh hot red chiles

½ cup chopped shallot

3 tablespoons fish sauce

3 tablespoons lime juice

3 tablespoons crushed palm sugar

4 ounces boneless
pork tenderloin, cut in strips

½ cup chopped dry tofu

2 tablespoons chopped
cilantro leaves

¼ cup chopped Thai
pickled garlic cloves

1 cup mung bean sprouts,
rinsed and drained

¼ cup chopped Chinese chives

*Look for the ones sold in small
bunches; they'll be easier to fry.

Thai Crispy Rice Noodles: *Mee Krob*

We all know the satisfying crunch of deep-fried noodles as restaurant fare or something you find in the processed-food aisle. With a skillet or wok, some oil, and a bit of heat, you can make this delicious crispy noodle dish at home.

1. Put the oil in a skillet or flat-bottomed wok over high heat. When the oil temperature reaches 375 degrees put in half the noodles. The action moves quickly here! When the noodles are puffed

and brown, about 1 minute, remove them and drain. Repeat with the other batch. Set aside. Note that different brands of noodles will bunch up in different ways and that some may require turning over in the hot oil. Whatever you do, don't serve raw rice noodles—make sure they're browned nicely.

2. In a clean, empty wok or skillet on high heat, add the 2 tablespoons of oil and when it gets very hot, mix in the dried shrimp and Chinese sausage. Cook and stir until the edges of the sausage start to brown, about 2 minutes.

3. Mix in the garlic, hot chiles, and shallot and cook, stirring, until the garlic starts to brown at the edges, about 2 minutes.

4. Add the fish sauce, lime juice, and palm sugar and cook and stir until the sugar has dissolved, about 1 minute.

5. Mix in the pork, tofu, cilantro, and pickled garlic and cook and stir until the pork is browned, about 4 minutes.

6. Mix in the bean sprouts and chives and cook and stir until the sprouts are tender, about 2 minutes.

7. Assemble the dish by putting the noodles on their respective serving plates and covering them with the stir-fried meat and vegetable.

Serve right away or it will become a soggy mess.

¼ cup Thai or Vietnamese fish sauce

2 tablespoons lime juice

¼ cup sugar

2 tablespoons crushed and finely chopped fresh garlic

1 tablespoon chopped fresh red hot chile pepper

1 tablespoon Thai chile garlic paste

¼ cup water

1 tablespoon salt

16 ounces shrimp, peeled and deveined

1 cup sliced shallot

1 cup chopped fresh tomato

¼ cup chopped cilantro

¼ cup chopped fresh mint leaves

½ cup crushed cashew nuts

6 ounces bean thread noodles, cooked, rinsed, and drained

Thai Noodle Salad: *Yum Woonsen*

In a hot climate like Thailand, there has to be something cool to eat that's not a sweet. Salads are the answer. This one manages to put the distinctive taste of Thailand on a single refreshing and intensely flavored plate.

1. Combine the fish sauce, lime juice, sugar, garlic, hot pepper, chile garlic paste, and ¼ cup water and mix until the sugar has dissolved. Let stand in the refrigerator until the flavors have combined, about 60 minutes, stirring as necessary to ensure the sugar fully dissolves.

2. Bring 2 quarts of water and the salt to a boil in a large pot and add the shrimp. Cook, stirring occasionally, until the meat turns opaque, about 1 minute. Drain shrimp and set aside, letting shrimp cool at least 10 minutes before proceeding.

3. Toss the cooked shrimp, shallot, tomato, cilantro, mint, and cashews together and make sure they're evenly combined.

4. To assemble the dish, put a bed of cooked noodles on a serving plate, heap some of the tossed shrimp and vegetable mixture over it, and finally pour the fish sauce mixture on top as a dressing.

Serve right away.

DON'T THROW THAT OIL AWAY!

THERE ISN'T ALL THAT MUCH deep-frying in this book; just a handful of recipes with a base of crispy noodles. Even so, I urge you to buy good-quality oil and take care of it. When you fry in peanut oil, you should have no problem getting it hot enough for good results without burning. And when you're finished, skim it or strain it and save it to use again.

This isn't as hard as it sounds. You can either run it through a paper coffee filter or one of those steel mesh skimmers that are sold to remove the surface scum from stock. You'll be left with clean oil that you can use again for any recipe that calls for deep-frying.

SINGAPORE

Fried Curry Noodles

Sometimes called Singapore Fried Noodles, this dish, like so many things in Singapore, combines elements from East and West to make something unique. In this case, the stir-frying technique is from China, the rice noodles are from Southeast Asia, and the curry powder is from Britain, Jamaica, or India, depending on who you ask and what variety of powder or paste you choose.

In this recipe, the kind of curry you add makes a big difference. American supermarket curry powder will give you a mild dish; Indian market curry paste will offer a bit more complexity and perhaps more heat. Chileheads can use Jamaican curry powder; this will give the dish a blast of heat and a brilliant yellow color. Taste! Think! Experiment!

1. Soak the rice noodles in hot water until they soften and begin to separate, about 15 minutes. Drain and set aside.

2. Put a wok or large skillet on high heat and make sure that it's really hot. You won't get real stir-frying without the heat. Add the oil, curry, and fish sauce and stir until they are well mixed, about 3 minutes.

3. Mix in the chicken and cook and stir until the pink color is gone, about 1 minute. If it takes longer, your pot isn't hot enough—don't be bashful!

MAKES 2 SERVINGS

8 ounces thin rice noodles

2 tablespoons peanut oil

2 tablespoons hot curry paste*

1 tablespoon Thai or Vietnamese fish sauce

½ pound boneless chicken thighs cut into thin strips

1 egg, beaten

1 cup mung bean sprouts, rinsed and drained

½ cup red and/or green bell pepper strips

1 tablespoon chopped fresh hot red chile pepper

2 tablespoons chopped scallions

*Alternatively, use 1 tablespoon Indian or Jamaican curry powder + 1 additional tablespoon peanut oil

4. Add the egg to the hot pan a few splashes at a time and keep stirring. The result should be little bits of cooked scrambled egg.

5. Mix in the bean sprouts, pepper strips, hot pepper, and scallions and cook and stir until the peppers and sprouts have wilted, about 4 minutes.

6. Add the noodles and cook and stir until they're coated with the curry mixture, about 1 minute. Stir with tongs instead of a spoon to make sure that all the ingredients are evenly distributed.

Serve right away.

MYANMAR (BURMA)

MAKES 2 SERVINGS

3 tablespoons crushed
and chopped garlic

1 cup chopped onion

2 tablespoons chopped
fresh ginger

1 teaspoon *belacan* or
dried shrimp paste

2 tablespoons peanut
oil + 2 tablespoons peanut
oil for frying

8 ounces boneless chicken
breast or thigh meat, cut
into dice-sized pieces

2 teaspoons red chile powder

1 teaspoon salt

3½ cups coconut
milk (2 14½ ounce cans)

8 ounces dried Asian egg noodles,
cooked, rinsed, and drained

Chicken Curry with Noodles: *Panthe Kaukswe*

It wasn't so long ago that *curry* was a culinary dirty word. It lumped all those spicy stews from South and Southeast Asia into a single group. More recently though, *curry*—originally an old English word for stew—has come to be a clear way to describe a distinct cooking technique: braising using a highly spiced cooking liquid. In this version from Burma (I know! It's Mayanmar now . . .), chicken is cooked with coconut milk and fermented shrimp paste and served with noodles. A distinct take on a familiar theme.

1. Combine the garlic, onion, ginger, shrimp paste, and 2 table-spoons of oil in a food processor and purée into a paste. This is best done in a sequence of pulses that take about 4 minutes. There should be no lumps in the paste afterward.

2. Put the remaining oil in a wok or large pot over medium heat and add the garlic/onion paste. Cook, stirring frequently, until it turns golden and the raw taste is gone, about 20 minutes.

3. Mix in the chicken and chile powder, continuing to stir fre-quently until the chicken is cooked through, about 10 minutes.

4. Add the coconut milk and cook with frequent stirring until the liquid is very hot, about 5 minutes. Then shut the heat off right away.

5. To assemble the dish, put the cooked egg noodles at the bottom of the serving bowls and ladle the hot soup mixture over them.

Serve immediately; if you don't, that coconut flavor will vanish.

Curried Fish Soup: *Mohinga*

I know all about fancy fish—salmon, tuna, swordfish, flounder. I also know that a typical person in Burma isn't going to eat them. A fish dish there is much more likely to be made with the humble catfish. This has its advantages; catfish are easily farmed in fresh water and are unlikely to be overfished the way that those tuna and

MAKES 4 SERVINGS

4 cups chopped onion

¼ cup chopped garlic

1 teaspoon belacan or dried shrimp paste

(continued on page 174)

1 teaspoon ground turmeric

3 tablespoons chopped fresh ginger

2 tablespoons sliced hot
red chile pepper

¼ cup peanut oil

8 cups water

1½ pounds catfish fillets,
cut into 1-inch pieces*

3 tablespoons fish sauce

2 lemongrass stalks, each
about 6 inches long, slit in half

8 ounces dry rice noodles,
soaked, rinsed, and drained

¼ cup chopped cilantro

1 lime, cut in quarters

2 hard cooked eggs, halved

*Substitute tilapia if you must.

swordfish are. All I ask is that you have no fear—the catfish will be delicious, I promise.

1. Combine the onion, garlic, shrimp paste, turmeric, ginger, and pepper in a blender or food processor and process until you have a thick paste with no large lumps, about 2 minutes. Pulsing will make this go much more easily.

2. Put the oil in a large pot over medium-low heat and add the onion and garlic mixture. Cook, stirring frequently, until it turns medium-brown and the raw taste is gone, about 45 minutes. You may have to lower the heat a bit during cooking to make sure the mixture doesn't burn.

3. Add the 8 cups of water, increase the heat to high, and bring the liquid to a boil. Add the fish, fish sauce, and lemongrass. Reduce the heat to medium-low and simmer with occasional stirring until the fish is cooked, about 20 minutes. Discard the lemongrass.

4. To assemble the dish, put the soaked noodles in serving bowls, ladle the hot soup mixture over it, and top with the cilantro and cooked egg wedges. Squeeze some of the lime over it for an extra shot of flavor.

Note: In Myanmar, the dish is often topped with slices of Chinese crullers called *yau jah guai*. It might seem odd to garnish a noodle dish with doughnuts, but I assure you it's authentic.

Beef and Noodle Soup: *Khow Suey*

Myanmar is a place so exotic, we rarely encounter its food. *Khow suey*, the country's classic noodle soup, tells the story well, though; noodles from China and curry from India combine into flavors strong enough to make you feel ready for any jungle trek.

1. Put the oil in a wok or large skillet on high heat and add the coriander, cumin, red chile powder, salt, and turmeric and cook and stir until the spices are coated with the oil, about 1 minute.

2. Mix in the beef and cook and stir until it begins to brown, about 5 minutes.

3. Reduce the heat to medium and mix in the garlic, ginger, lemongrass, and onion and cook, stirring frequently, until the garlic has begun to brown at the edges and the onion is translucent, about 20 minutes.

4. Add the 6 cups of water to the mixture and simmer uncovered with occasional stirring until the meat is tender and about half the liquid has evaporated, about 60 minutes. If it evaporates more quickly, reduce the heat a bit.

5. Mix in the coconut milk and stir until it's evenly distributed. Simmer, stirring occasionally, until the liquid thickens, about 5 minutes.

(continued on page 176)

MAKES 2 SERVINGS

3 tablespoons peanut oil

1 teaspoon ground coriander

1 teaspoon ground cumin

1 teaspoon red chile powder

1 teaspoon salt

½ teaspoon ground turmeric

½ pound beef chuck stew meat, cut in dice-sized cubes*

3 tablespoons crushed and chopped garlic

2 tablespoons minced fresh ginger

2 tablespoons finely chopped lemongrass

2 cups chopped onion

6 cups water

1½ cups coconut milk

8 ounces dried Chinese egg noodles, cooked, rinsed, and drained

2 hard-cooked eggs, sliced

½ cup thinly sliced red onion

2 tablespoons chopped fresh cilantro

¼ cup deep-fried onion

*In Mayanmar, they might use chicken or mutton instead.

6. Assemble the dish by placing a serving of noodles in a large bowl, ladling the beef mixture over it, and then topping with half the sliced eggs, red onion, cilantro, and deep-fried onion.

Serve right away.

INDONESIA

MAKES 2 SERVINGS

4 cups water

½ pound boneless
chicken thigh meat

1 teaspoon salt

3 tablespoons peanut oil

8 ounces thin Asian egg noodles,
cooked, rinsed, and drained

¼ cup soy sauce

3 eggs beaten

2 cups sliced napa cabbage

1 cup sliced baby bok choy

¼ cup chopped scallions

¼ cup deep-fried onions

1 teaspoon ground white pepper

Fried Egg Noodles: *Mie Goreng Jawa*

Here's Indonesia's contribution to the world of fried noodles. It's easily identifiable as part of the same Asian-noodle-cuisine family, with its soy sauce, egg, and typical greens. It's also unique, with its precooked chicken. And while the name means "fried noodles from Java," I don't think you'd wash them down with a cup of coffee. That being said, you can find them everywhere in Indonesia.

1. Bring the water to a boil in a medium pot and add the chicken and salt. Reduce the heat to medium-low and simmer uncovered until the chicken is done, about 10 minutes. Let cool, set the chicken aside, and separately reserve the broth.

2. Put a wok or large skillet on high heat and add the oil, cooked noodles, and soy sauce. Cook and stir until the noodles are coated with the sauce, about 2 minutes.

3. Mix in the reserved chicken meat and 1 cup of the reserved chicken broth. Cook and stir until the broth starts to boil, about 3 minutes.

4. Push the noodles and meat to the side of the pan and slowly pour the beaten eggs into the puddle of boiling liquid at the bottom. Give the broth and egg mixture an occasional stir to help form small pieces.

5. Toss the cooked egg with the noodles and mix in the cabbage, bok choy, and scallions. Cook and stir until the cabbage is tender, about 3 minutes.

6. Top with the fried onions and pepper and serve right away.

MAKES 2 SERVINGS

½ cup chopped shallot or red onion

3 cloves fresh garlic

¼ cup cashew nut pieces

½ teaspoon salt

1 tablespoon chopped fresh ginger

1 teaspoon whole coriander seeds

1 teaspoon whole cumin seeds

½ teaspoon turmeric powder

3 tablespoons peanut oil

½ pound boneless chicken thigh or breast meat, cut in thin strips

2 cups chicken broth

1 stalk lemongrass, about 4 inches long, shredded

2 cups water

1 cup coconut milk

2 bunches fine rice noodles (about 6 ounces), soaked and drained

2 tablespoons chopped scallion

½ cup mung bean sprouts

Noodles in a Seasoned Broth: *Soto Ayam*

Soto ayam is Indonesia's contribution to that great noodle subcategory, chicken noodle soup. In the tradition of this region, there's a paste of spices, rice noodles, and a dose of hot sauce added at the table.

1. Put the shallot, garlic, cashews, salt, ginger, coriander, cumin, and turmeric in a food processor and blend into a coarse paste, about 2 minutes. Set aside.

2. Put the oil in a large pot over medium heat and mix in the spice blend, stirring until they're combined, about 2 minutes.

3. Mix in the chicken, stirring frequently until the meat is cooked on the outside and coated with the spice mixture, about 10 minutes.

4. Add the broth, lemongrass, and water and simmer covered, stirring occasionally, until the chicken is cooked through and tender, about 30 minutes.

5. Add the coconut milk and cook and stir until the broth is hot again, about 2 minutes.

6. To assemble the dish, put half the soaked noodles, scallion, and bean sprouts in a large bowl and ladle the soup over it.

Note: This dish is traditionally served with lime wedges and *sambal*, the Indonesian chile sauce.

TIBET

Handmade Noodles in Broth: *Thenthuk*

When did Tibetan appear on the American immigrant-cuisine landscape? Ten years ago, there were a couple of restaurants in Manhattan. Today, there's a whole Little Tibet in Queens, New York, and a thriving Tibetan community in Vermont, a place that almost nobody associates with immigrants or ethnic cuisines. One of the dishes you'll be offered in Tibetan restaurants is this comforting soup with big, chewy noodles.

1. Put the oil and onion in a large pot over medium heat and cook and stir until the onion becomes tender and translucent, about 20 minutes.

2. Mix in the garlic, ginger, and beef and cook, stirring occasionally, until the meat is well browned, about 20 minutes.

3. Raise the heat to high and add the tomato, daikon, soy sauce, beef broth, and water. When the liquid comes to a boil, reduce the heat to medium-low, cover the pot, and simmer with occasional stirring until the meat becomes tender, about 45 minutes.

4. While the meat broth is cooking, make the noodle dough by putting the flour in a large bowl and mixing in the ¾ cup of water. Work it with a spoon until it comes together and can be kneaded by hand. If it's too dry, add water, 1 tablespoon at a time, until it's

2 tablespoons peanut oil

2 cups chopped onion

3 tablespoons crushed and chopped fresh garlic

2 tablespoons crushed and chopped peeled fresh ginger

1 pound boneless beef chuck cut into 1-inch cubes*

1 cup chopped tomato

2 cups peeled and thinly sliced daikon

2 tablespoons soy sauce

4 cups beef broth

4 cups water + ¾ cup for the dough

1½ cups flour

¼ cup chopped cilantro

2 tablespoons chopped scallion greens

3 cups fresh spinach or 1 package frozen leaf spinach (about 10 ounces), defrosted

*If you can find yak or mutton, they'll give a more authentic flavor, but beef is fine. Yak and mutton need a longer cooking time in step 3, though; simmer for 90 minutes instead.

pliable. If it's too soft, add flour, 1 tablespoon at a time, until you have a kneadable dough.

5. Knead the dough until it springs back when you stick your thumb into it. Cover the dough with a towel and let it rest for 20 minutes.

6. After the dough has rested, cut it into quarters and then roll it out into long strips about 1-inch wide. Then either press the strips flat with a rolling pin or use a pasta machine at its thickest setting.

7. Raise the heat of the soup to high. When the liquid is boiling again, tear the dough strips into 2-inch-long pieces and toss them in the soup one at a time. Every noodle will wind up a different length and shape—don't sweat it. Reduce the heat to medium-low, and simmer, stirring occasionally, until the noodles are cooked, about 7 minutes.

8. Mix in the cilantro, scallions, and spinach and remove from the heat.

Serve right away.

LITTLE TIBET IS BIGGER THAN YOU THINK

I'D HEARD RUMORS of a Tibetan restaurant in New York City for years, and I think I may have walked by it once or twice. You'd think that a guy like me would drop everything, dash right in, and eat up a storm. It's just that in a place like the Big Apple, you can't really do that; after all, there might be ten other places (and cuisines) you'd want to try on the same block. It kills me to admit it, but self-control is called for here.

So when I was searching for Tibetan restaurants and recipes for this book and wound up watching a video of a Miss Tibet beauty pageant instead, it took me a while to get used to the idea that there were now enough Tibetans in the country to make up a "Tibetan community," with beauty queens, service organizations, and yes, restaurants.

That video showed a woman heading down a flight of stairs and into a shop that sold Tibetan books, music, and knickknacks. Signs she walked passed made it clear that they were in Jackson Heights, the legendary Queens, New York, immigrant neighborhood. Since I spent almost a decade living a few short blocks from the scene in the video, I felt familiar enough with the area to scoot right over.

With the help of a sympathetic police officer, I found those stairs, headed down, and to my amazement there

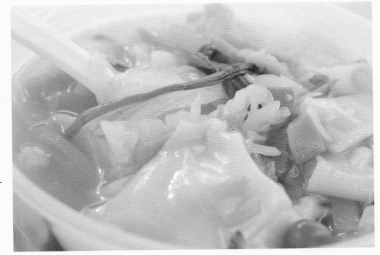

was the store, and standing at the counter was the very woman in the video, a big smile on her face and a bag of Tibetan dried cheese in her hands. That cheese piqued my curiosity—it looked like bread crumbs to me—but I was looking for noodles and this store didn't have them.

Outside, I found a cluster of Tibetan and Nepali restaurants—okay, they were really more snack shop than restaurant—right by a closed-off street with chairs and tables. Here, on a brisk November morning, people sat and sipped from what any New Yorker would recognize as takeout coffee cups. Since I'm always ready for a cup of coffee, I walked up to a vendor and ordered one. "No coffee here," I was told, "only Tibetan butter tea. How much salt do you take?" Mustering every last bit of courage, I ordered the mysterious concoction.

Removing the tab on the plastic lid of the container, I saw a liquid that looked like tea with milk. I was sure that a million British truck drivers were at that very moment consuming the same thing. That is, until I tasted it. Salty and buttery, this strong black tea had been flavored with milk, butter, and salt. It was a flavor combination I never had before, something like liquid, tea-flavored popcorn. Like rattlesnake chili, it was a taste you might read about a million times and still not believe it actually exists. Each time I sipped, I shook my head in amazement. Tea, salt, and butter . . . in a cup . . . one liquid . . . looking for all the world like takeout tea, but in reality, the unique taste of a country that was very far away.

This was all well and good, but what I really wanted were noodles. Tibetan *thenthuk* (page 183), to be precise. The tea vendor offered them with chicken, beef, or vegetable. I chose chicken, and while I was waiting the vendor told me that the name *thenthuk* (also spelled *then thuk* and *then tuk*) means "pull-drop" in Tibetan. "Pull-drop" describes how the noodles are made. First, you pull a bit of dough from a blob, and then you drop it in the boiling broth. It was his opinion that they might not really be noodles at all, and this sent me deep into the land of pointless food thought. They were made from a kneaded wheat flour dough, but not cut evenly or pressed through a die. Would this make them dropped dumplings, instead? When he handed me my container of *thenthuk*, it was something that any Italian would call pasta without a second thought—that alone meant that it was a noodle as far as I was concerned.

There was the fantasy—a lavishly decorated restaurant with charming servers and beautiful dishes—and the reality . . . a plastic container, paper napkins, and outdoor seating: 21st-century street food. My disposable tub was probably more authentic than any exotic decor could possibly be. With a cold wind and low winter sun, I might as well have been in Tibet. Yes, faraway Tibet; that is, until I tasted my *thenthuk*. What I had were noodles, vegetables, and bits of chicken in broth. Blindfolded, I'd swear it was Grandma's chicken soup from anywhere in northern Europe. Jewish penicillin with somewhat funny-shaped noodles and slices of white radish that almost could have passed for potato.

The broth was golden. It was that mild liquid chicken you could find anywhere. There wasn't much salt; after all, there was enough salt in the tea to keep a person going. And the vegetables? Slices of carrot, daikon, a few peas, and some spinach leaves. Add to that some bits of chicken that had given up their flavor to the soup long ago. What really filled the container though, was the *thenthuk*, thick, dull white, and nothing like any dropped dumpling. They were solid, rough-cut noodles—no doubt about it. It all added up to a meal of some amazingly mild food in one of New York's most exotic neighborhoods.

There were also tiny containers of hot sauce; one was brown vinegar with sliced bits of green chile and the other was the red, gloppy stuff that everybody knows. Grandma would have thought they were a poor substitute for horseradish, but otherwise, the whole thing was the tamest immigrant-cuisine dish I'd ever tasted. Something that could be enjoyed by people who feared tacos and chow mein. This is what they ate in far-off Shangri-La? It was the perfect entry-level adventure eating dish, washed down with butter tea—the most alien taste in all of New York City.

What a combo.

NEPAL

Fried Noodles: *Chow Chow*

Wedged into a corner between Tibet and India and almost totally walled in by huge mountain ranges, Nepal takes its culinary influences from the south, with a love of curries and chiles, and the north, with a reliance on soy sauce and bean sprouts.

In a remote place like Nepal, this dish is typically made with Chinese dried noodles—the ones called lo mein in much of the world. It's not limited to that, though. You can just as easily find cooks using spaghetti in the same dish. Both of those noodles have a way of traveling to unexpected places, so this should be no surprise.

1. Put a wok or large skillet on high heat and add the oil, fenugreek, turmeric, peppercorns, and pepper and cook and stir until the spices are coated with the oil and begin to pop, about 1 minute.

2. Mix in the soy sauce and onion and cook and stir until the onion is translucent, about 4 minutes.

3. Mix in the carrot, garlic, ginger, hot chiles, and bell pepper strips and cook and stir until the carrot starts to become tender, about 4 minutes.

4. Mix in the lamb meat and cook and stir until it's barely cooked, about 3 minutes.

MAKES 2 SERVINGS

3 tablespoons peanut oil

1 teaspoon fenugreek seeds

1 teaspoon ground turmeric

½ teaspoon Sichuan peppercorns

1 teaspoon freshly ground pepper

2 tablespoons soy sauce

1 cup chopped onion

½ cup carrot strips

2 tablespoons crushed and chopped garlic

1 tablespoon finely chopped ginger

1 tablespoon chopped fresh hot red chile peppers

1 cup green bell pepper strips

8 ounces boneless lamb meat, cut into thin strips

8 ounces dry Chinese noodles or spaghetti, cooked, rinsed, and drained

1 cup mung bean sprouts, rinsed and drained

½ cup chopped scallion greens

5. Add the cooked noodles and toss with the other ingredients until the noodles are hot and everything else is evenly distributed, about 3 minutes.

6. Mix in the bean sprouts and scallion greens and cook and stir until the sprouts are tender, about 1 minute.

Serve right away. Nepalese restaurants typically offer ketchup on the side.

INDIA

Instant Masala Noodles

MAKES 1 SERVING

1 tablespoon peanut oil

1 cup chopped onion

1 tablespoon chopped garlic

½ cup chopped red and/or green bell pepper (you can buy presliced frozen mixed pepper strips in the supermarket freezer section)

1 tablespoon chopped fresh hot red chile pepper

½ teaspoon whole mustard seeds

½ teaspoon ground garam masala powder

½ teaspoon whole cumin seed

¼ teaspoon *asafoetida* (also called *hing*)

2 cups water

1 packet of instant ramen noodles, including the broth mix

Noodles aren't a traditional Indian food, but they've found their way into the nation's diet. One of the most popular forms in India is instant ramen. In addition to the same chicken and seafood varieties that Americans are offered are a range of flavors of varying degrees of spiciness (see pages 98 and 194). Those instant packs fit in with one Indian food tradition perfectly—the idea that anything can be improved with a bit more seasoning.

Oh yes . . . one serving? Well, people don't usually make instant noodles for a crowd, and prepared as is for one they can be pretty depressing. This is a good compromise.

1. Put the oil, onion, garlic, bell pepper, and hot pepper in a pan over medium-high heat and cook and stir until the onion begins to brown at the edges, about 15 minutes.

2. Mix in the mustard seeds, garam masala, cumin, and *asafoetida* and cook and stir until the spices are coated with oil, about 3 minutes.

3. Increase the heat to high and add 2 cups of water. When the water comes to a boil, add the noodle seasoning packet and the noodles themselves. Reduce the heat to a simmer and cook until the noodles are tender, about 2 minutes.

Serve right away with a good chutney or Indian pickle.

FIVE (MORE) THINGS TO DO WITH INSTANT RAMEN

WITH ALL THE THINGS YOU CAN DO with instant ramen, some people treat it as an ingredient rather than a dish. These five suggestions are just a beginning.

1. Season the broth with soy sauce, fish sauce, miso, or curry paste. Add one teaspoon per serving of any *one* of these. Don't rule out hot sauces—anything from peppers in vinegar to Tabasco is a possibility. I personally find hot mustard to be a treat (use those packets they give out at Chinese takeout shops). You can combine these condiments with any of the add-ins that follow.

2. Add fresh vegetables. Those white mung bean sprouts are a traditional Asian ingredient and a good start. Toss a handful of sprouts into the boiling broth and you'll add nutrition and texture with very little effort. Napa cabbage requires a bit of work to cut into strips, but with its bright green color it does a good job of jazzing up the bowl. Shredded carrots are great too. If you buy them already shredded in the supermarket produce section, I promise not to tell anybody. Frozen peas or snow peas make a nice, easy addition as well.

3. You can add an egg by breaking it into the boiling broth before you add the noodles. Just let it sit in the hot liquid for about 1 minute, then give it a few stirs to disperse it. You can add slices of hard-boiled egg, too. You can also top a bowl of ramen with a fried egg, although it will mean getting a second pot dirty, which kind of defeats the purpose of eating instant ramen in the first place.

4. Fish or seafood may seem a bit lavish, but a small can of tuna or salmon added to a bowl of ramen can give it a shot of protein and flavor. Frozen shrimp or seafood mix can be stirred into

the broth after you add the seasoning pack and before you add the noodles. I suggest about half a cup per pack of ramen.

5. For me, the toughest addition is meat. Hawaiians will put pieces of Spam in theirs. If that's not to your liking, how about a bit of precooked bacon? The thin slices of beef and lamb sold for hot pot in Chinese and Korean markets are great if you find them fresh and in small quantities.

(*Note:* Do not under any circumstances refreeze packaged frozen meat slices that have been defrosted!)

Don't be afraid to mix and match—a pack of ramen with bean sprouts, an egg, and some hot mustard is an awful lot better than a pack of ramen all by itself.

MAKES 2 SERVINGS

2 tablespoons peanut oil

1 tablespoon whole cumin seed

2 teaspoons garam masala powder

2 tablespoons ginger garlic paste

1 tablespoon soy sauce

1 cup chopped red onion

2 tablespoons chopped
fresh green hot pepper

1 cup thinly sliced carrot

1 cup thinly sliced napa cabbage

1 cup mung bean sprouts

2 tablespoons tomato ketchup

12 ounces fresh lo mein
noodles or 8 ounces spaghetti,
cooked, rinsed, and drained

2 tablespoons sliced scallions

Vegetarian Hakka Noodles

What happens when a fusion dish morphs so much that it no longer resembles the cuisine from which it came? Vegetarian Hakka noodles are held forth as a dish from the Hakka region of China that has been re-created in India's Chinatowns for at least a century. It's just that somehow, they've become Indian. Actually, I thought that at least the noodles themselves were Chinese—that is, until I saw Indian home cooks using spaghetti and adding ketchup.

1. Put a wok or large skillet on high heat and add the oil and cumin seed. Cook and stir until the seeds start to brown, about 2 minutes.

2. Mix in the garam masala powder, ginger garlic paste, and soy sauce and cook and stir until these ingredients combine with the hot oil, about 1 minute.

3. Add the onion, pepper, carrot, and cabbage and cook, stirring frequently, until the carrot is tender, about 5 minutes.

4. Mix in the bean sprouts and ketchup and continue to stir frequently until the bean sprouts are tender and the ketchup combines with the sauce, about 2 minutes.

5. Add the cooked noodles and toss until they're hot, coated with sauce, and the vegetables are evenly distributed, about 3 minutes.

6. Remove from the heat, toss with the scallions, and serve right away.

Coconut Rice Noodles *(Sevai)*

Yes, there are noodles in India that aren't instant or imported. These, called *sevai*, are from the deep south and are similar to the rice noodles you see all over Asia. Similar or not, when you combine them with these distinctly Indian flavors, there's no question about their origin.

1. Soak the *sevai* by putting them in a large bowl and pouring very hot water over them until they're barely covered. Cover the bowl (a large plate works fine here) and let stand for 15 minutes. Drain the *sevai*, rinse them in cold water, and drain again. Set aside.

2. Put the oil in a skillet over high heat and add the mustard seed, *urad dhal,* and salt. Cook and stir until the mustard seeds start popping, about 1 minute.

3. Reduce the heat to medium and mix in the green and red chiles, coconut, *asafoetida*, cashews, and curry leaves and cook, stirring occasionally until the chiles become tender, about 5 minutes.

4. Mix in the soaked *sevai* and keep cooking with occasional stirring until the noodles have absorbed the flavors and the chiles and cashews are evenly distributed.

Serve right away.

4 ounces *sevai* (about 2 cups)

2 tablespoons peanut oil

1 teaspoon whole mustard seed

1 teaspoon *urad dhal*

1 teaspoon salt

1 tablespoon chopped
fresh green chiles

1 tablespoon chopped
fresh red chiles

½ cup shredded coconut
(frozen is easiest)

½ teaspoon ground
asafoetida (also called *hing*)

½ cup chopped cashew nuts

1 tablespoon fresh curry leaves

2 tablespoons *tukmaria* seeds (ask for *falooda* seeds)

4 ounces *sevai* (or fine rice noodles broken into small pieces) soaked in hot water, rinsed, and drained

½ cup rose syrup (look for the red liquid, *not* rose water)

4 cups whole milk

4 scoops (about 1 pint) *kulfi* or Indian ice cream

Noodles and Ice Cream Shake: *Falooda*

We know noodles. Mostly savory and sometimes sweet. But a drink? *Falooda* is easily the world's most popular noodle drink. You'll find it anywhere Indian or Pakistani snacks are sold—an ice cream shake with noodles.

Note that while this dish uses quite a few unique ingredients, you can find them all at any Indian grocery. Indeed, choosing between the flavors of Indian ice cream should be worth a trip in itself.

1. Soak the *tukmaria* seeds in 4 cups of warm water until tender, about 1 hour. Drain and set aside.

2. Put the soaked noodles and rose syrup at the bottom of 4 tall glasses.

3. Pour the milk over the noodle mixture.

4. Mix in a portion of the soaked *tukmaria* seeds.

5. Top each glass with a scoop of the ice cream.

Serve cold with a straw and a spoon. You can eat, drink, and lick a *falooda* all at the same time.

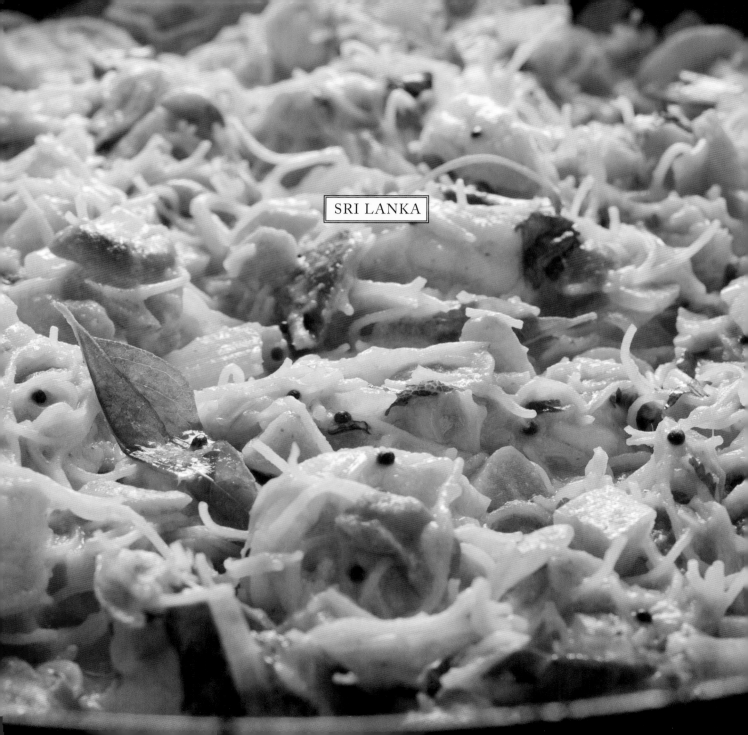

SRI LANKA

Tamil String Hopper Biryani: *Idiyappam Biryani*

MAKES 4 SERVINGS

String hoppers are a Tamil favorite, found in Tamil regions of both India and Sri Lanka. This dish is called a biryani for its similarity to the classic Indian rice dish; you may need a moment to see that what you've got here are really noodles.

1. Combine the ginger garlic paste, chile, turmeric, and coriander in a large bowl. Make sure there are no lumps of spice powder.

2. Add the shrimp, mix until it's coated with the spice paste, and let marinate in the refrigerator for at least 15 minutes.

3. Put the oil, mustard seeds, saffron, and cloves in a wok or large skillet over high heat and cook and stir until the mustard seeds start to pop, about 2 minutes.

4. Add the cashew nuts and cook and stir until they begin to brown, about 3 minutes.

5. Mix in the carrot, cabbage, leek, curry leaves, and onion, reduce the heat to medium, and cook, stirring frequently, until the vegetables are tender, about 15 minutes.

6. Mix in the marinated shrimp and cook and stir until the shrimp turns opaque, about 3 minutes.

¼ cup ginger garlic paste

1 teaspoon hot chile powder

1 teaspoon ground turmeric

1 teaspoon ground coriander

1 pound shelled and deveined shrimp

2 tablespoons peanut oil

1 teaspoon whole mustard seeds

¼ teaspoon saffron threads

2 whole cloves

½ cup cashew nut pieces

½ cup chopped carrot

1 cup chopped cabbage

½ cup sliced leek greens

2 tablespoons fresh curry leaves

1 cup chopped red onion

½ cup yogurt

2 cups *sevai* Indian rice noodles (or fine rice noodles broken into small pieces), dry

2 tablespoons chopped cilantro leaves

1 tablespoon chopped mint leaves

7. Mix in the yogurt and cook and stir until it combines with the liquid at the bottom of the pan to form a sauce, about 3 minutes. If there's no liquid after the yogurt has been added, mix in 1 cup of water.

8. Mix in the noodle pieces and cook with frequent stirring until they absorb the liquid and become tender, about 3 minutes. If the pan dries out before this happens, add water, ¼ cup at a time, until they soften.

9. Toss with the cilantro and mint leaves and serve right away.

PAKISTAN

MAKES 4 SERVINGS

Spicy Spaghetti with Meat Sauce: *Keema Khousa*

2 tablespoons peanut oil

1 teaspoon ground cumin

1 teaspoon ground coriander

½ teaspoon ground turmeric

1 teaspoon salt

2 tablespoons ginger garlic paste

2 tablespoons chopped fresh green chile

2 cups chopped onion

1 pound ground beef

¼ cup plain yogurt

1 cup canned crushed tomato

1 pound spaghetti, cooked and drained

Here's Pakistan's version of spaghetti and meat sauce. Something that looks a bit like the famous dish from Bologna, Italy (page 119), but with a twist or two reflecting the local flavors.

1. Put the oil in a heavy pot over medium heat and mix in the cumin, coriander, turmeric, and salt. Cook and stir until the spices are coated with the oil, about 1 minute.

2. Mix in the ginger garlic paste and cook and stir until the pastes have combined with the oil and spices, about 1 minute.

3. Add the chile and onions and keep cooking, stirring occasionally until the onions have absorbed the spices and become translucent, about 10 minutes.

4. Mix in the ground beef and use the back of a spoon to keep breaking it into the smallest pieces possible. Cook until the beef and onions are both browned, about 20 minutes.

5. Add the yogurt and tomatos, reduce the heat to medium-low, and cook, stirring occasionally until all the flavors have combined, about 20 minutes.

6. Finally, add the cooked spaghetti to the pot and toss so that all the ingredients are evenly distributed. Serve right away.

AFGHANISTAN

1 CUP 240

Spaghetti with Meat Sauce and Beans: *Aush*

In a way, this dish from Afghanistan isn't so different from Cincinnati chili served over spaghetti. But, with the yogurt and mint, it also strongly recalls its country of origin. Then again, meat sauce is as universal as noodles, right?

1. Bring 8 cups of water to a boil over high heat and add the tablespoon of salt, split peas, chickpeas, and red kidney beans. (If you're using canned kidney beans and/or chickpeas, add them after the yellow splits have cooked for 45 minutes.) Lower the heat to a simmer, cover, and cook, stirring occasionally, until the beans become tender, about 60 minutes.

2. While the beans are simmering, cook the oil and onion in a large skillet over high heat. Cook and stir until the onion starts to brown, about 5 minutes.

3. Mix in the beef and use a wooden spoon to break up the clumps of meat. Keep cooking, stirring occasionally, until the meat has browned, about 10 more minutes.

4. Mix the tomato paste, salt, and pepper into the meat mixture and reduce the heat to medium-low. Continue to cook until the tomato is absorbed by the meat, about 15 more minutes. Set aside until the dish is ready to be assembled.

MAKES 4 SERVINGS

1 tablespoon salt + 1 teaspoon salt

1 cup soaked and rinsed yellow split peas

1 cup soaked and rinsed chickpeas*

1 cup soaked and rinsed red kidney beans*

2 cups chopped spinach (or 1 cup chopped frozen spinach, thawed)

¼ cup peanut oil

1 cup chopped onion

1 pound ground beef

2 tablespoons tomato paste

1 teaspoon freshly ground pepper

1 pound spaghetti, dry

1 cup plain Greek-style yogurt

1 tablespoon chopped, fresh mint leaves

1 teaspoon red chile powder

2 tablespoons chopped cilantro

*You can substitute rinsed canned chickpeas and kidney beans here, just be sure to rinse and drain them before you add them in, and note the timing change in step 1.

5. Back to the bean pot . . . After the beans are cooked, add 4 cups of water, increase the heat to high, and bring to a boil. Add the spaghetti, lower the heat to medium-low, and simmer until the spaghetti is just about cooked, about 9 minutes. Then mix in the spinach. When it's wilted, about 1 minute later, drain any excess liquid, then mix in the cooked meat mixture and toss until all the ingredients are evenly distributed. Remove from the heat.

6. While the spaghetti is cooking—yes, there's a third component—make the yogurt sauce by mixing the yogurt, mint, chile, and cilantro together in a large bowl. Set it aside until the dish is ready to be assembled.

7. Top the spaghetti, meat, and beans with the spiced yogurt mixture and serve right away.

UZBEKISTAN

Lamb, Vegetable, and Noodle Stew: *Lagman*

MAKES 4 SERVINGS

As a classic dish from Uzbekistan, *lagman* is comfort food from a very faraway place. Maybe it's all that garlic, but when you eat it, you get a cozy sense of the familiar and a taste of the exotic all at the very same time.

1. Put a heavy pot over medium heat and add the oil, black cumin seeds, cumin, coriander, chile flakes, salt, pepper, and bay leaves and cook and stir until the spices are coated with the oil, about 2 minutes.

2. Reduce the heat to medium-low and mix in the onion, garlic, carrot, and bell pepper and cook, stirring frequently, until the onion becomes translucent and the bell pepper becomes tender, about 20 minutes.

3. Add the lamb and continue to cook, stirring occasionally, until the meat is browned and the vegetables have become very soft, about 20 minutes.

4. Raise the heat to high, add the broth, potato, and tomato and bring to a boil. After the stew has boiled for 1 minute, reduce the heat to medium-low and cook, stirring occasionally, until the meat is tender and the onions have almost dissolved, about 40 minutes. If the mixture becomes too dry, add water, 1 cup at a time, to bring to a simmer again.

5. To serve, place a heap of cooked noodles or spaghetti at the bottom of each serving bowl and ladle the stew over the noodles.

¼ cup olive oil

1 tablespoon black cumin seeds

1 teaspoon ground cumin

1 teaspoon ground coriander

1 teaspoon dried chile flakes

1 teaspoon salt

1 teaspoon freshly ground pepper

2 bay leaves

2 cups chopped onion

¼ cup crushed and chopped fresh garlic

1 cup sliced carrot (we're going for disks here, not sticks)

1 cup chopped red bell pepper

1 pound boneless lamb stew meat, cut into dice-sized pieces

1 quart chicken broth (page 87)

1 cup chopped potato

1 cup chopped fresh tomato

1 pound dry lo mein or spaghetti, cooked, rinsed, and drained

MAKES 4 SERVINGS

8 ounces natural
unflavored beef jerky

1 tablespoon salt

8 ounces medium egg noodles

1 cup thinly sliced red onion

1 tablespoon whole cumin seeds

1 tablespoon butter

Dried Beef and Noodles: *Norin*

How is it that this combination of commonly available ingredients has become such a unique dish? Indeed, I spent so much time dwelling on Uzbek recipes for dried meat that I failed to notice that it was awfully similar to plain beef jerky. Just remember, you don't need cured mutton or horse for this dish; nomads might have used the meat of a variety of animals, but they used beef often enough. Jerky is just fine. And I assure you, 99.9 percent of Americans have never tasted anything like this dish, even if they know all the ingredients.

1. Bring 8 cups of water to a boil in a large saucepan over high heat and add the beef jerky. Stir a few times, reduce the heat to medium-low, and simmer, stirring ocasionally, until the meat is tender, about 15 minutes. Drain, reserving the cooking water, and set aside.

2. Cut the boiled jerky meat into matchstick-sized strips. Set aside.

3. Return the beef-cooking water to a boil and mix in the salt and noodles. Reduce the heat to medium-low and simmer, stirring frequently, until the noodles are tender, about 8 minutes. Drain.

4. Put the chopped cooked beef, cooked noodles, onion, cumin seed, and butter in a bowl and toss until all the ingredients are evenly distributed.

Serve right away.

UKRAINE

Noodle, Bacon, and Cottage Cheese Casserole: *Lokshyna, Zapechena z Syrom*

Let's not beat around the bush—this is a rich dish. It's food for people who work hard in a very harsh climate. Indeed, you can feel the winter winds howling across Siberia while you're cooking it. Eat it and you'll see that it can beat any blizzard.

1. Put the bacon in a large skillet over medium-high heat and cook, turning the bacon until it's browned on both sides, about 15 minutes. Reserve the bacon and its fat.

2. Preheat the oven to 375 degrees.

3. Combine the cooked noodles with the bacon and bacon fat in a large bowl. Toss together until the bacon is evenly distributed throughout the noodles.

4. Put the cottage cheese in a separate large bowl and mix in the white pepper, eggs, and cream, beating with a large, wooden spoon until everything is evenly combined, about 3 minutes.

5. Use half the butter to grease an ovenproof baking dish and then cover the bottom with about a third of the noodle and bacon mixture. Then cover that with half the cheese and egg mixture, then put in another third of the noodle and bacon mixture, cover the second third of the noodles with the remaining half of the

MAKES 6 SERVINGS

1 pound bacon, chopped

1 pound wide egg noodles, cooked and drained

1 pound whole milk cottage cheese

1 teaspoon ground white pepper

3 eggs

¼ cup heavy cream

¼ cup butter

¼ cup unseasoned dry breadcrumbs

cheese and egg mixture, and finally top with the remaining third of the noodles.

6. Sprinkle the breadcrumbs on top of the casserole and put bits of the remaining butter over the crumbs. Bake uncovered until the breadcrumbs have browned, about 35 minutes.

That's butter, noodles, cheese, noodles, cheese, noodles, breadcrumbs, and finally, butter. Whew!

Serve hot.

Note: No additional salt needed; the bacon will have plenty!

TURKEY

Noodles with Arugula, Walnuts, and Yogurt: *Rokali Eriste*

1 package (12 ounces) medium egg noodles

1 tablespoon salt

3 cups chopped fresh arugula

1 cup plain, whole milk Greek-style yogurt

1 cup walnut pieces

Just when you think you've seen every possible way that a pile of noodles can be served, you encounter a new cuisine and find them being prepared in a way you never would have guessed.

1. Bring 3 quarts of water to a boil in a large pot over high heat. Add the noodles and salt, reduce the heat to medium, and let cook uncovered, stirring occasionally, until the noodles begin to become tender, about 3 minutes.

2. Add the arugula and keep cooking until the noodles are fully cooked and the arugula is wilted, about 2 minutes. Drain and put on plates for serving.

3. Put a scoop of the yogurt and a handful of walnuts on top of the cooked noodles.

Serve right away.

Noodles with Mushrooms: *Mantarli Eriste*

MAKES 2 SERVINGS

There are times when you can throw a few ingredients in a pan, put them on top of a pile of noodles, and wind up with something far better than you ever expected. Indeed, this seems to be the whole idea of Turkish noodle cookery.

1. Put the olive oil, chile flakes, salt, pepper, and onion in a skillet over medium heat and cook, stirring frequently until the onion becomes tender, about 15 minutes.

2 tablespoons olive oil

1 teaspoon dried chile flakes

1 teaspoon salt

1 teaspoon freshly ground pepper

1 cup chopped onion

2 tablespoons crushed and chopped fresh garlic

2 cups fresh mushroom slices*

1 cup chopped fresh tomato

12 ounces wide egg noodles, cooked, drained, and tossed with 1 tablespoon butter

2 tablespoons chopped parsley

1 teaspoon lemon zest

*Plain white mushrooms are fine here, but try using shiitake or other varieties if you can.

2. Mix in the garlic and mushrooms, stirring occasionally until the mushrooms are cooked through, about 15 minutes.

3. Mix in the chopped tomato and cook, stirring occasionally until the tomato breaks down and its flavors combine with the other ingredients, about 20 minutes.

4. Put the buttered noodles on serving plates and cover with the cooked mushroom mixture. Sprinkle with the parsley and lemon zest.

Serve right away.

Note: You can make the mushroom mixture (steps 1–3) in advance and reheat before serving with the noodles.

SYRIA

MAKES 4 SERVINGS

2 cups plain yogurt

2 tablespoons crushed and chopped garlic

½ teaspoon of salt

2 tablespoons chopped parsley

1 tablespoon chopped mint leaves

1 pound *bucatini,* or thick spaghetti, cooked, rinsed in cold water, and drained

½ cup raw almonds

1 teaspoon paprika

Spaghetti with Yogurt Sauce: *Macarona bi Laban*

Spaghetti and yogurt? Really? Or more precisely, spaghetti with some great Middle Eastern flavors. It's a Syrian favorite.

1. Combine the yogurt, garlic, salt, parsley, and mint in a large bowl. Mix well, cover, and let stand in the refrigerator for at least 1 hour in order for the flavors to combine.

2. Add the cooked pasta and toss so that all the strands are coated evenly and the ingredients are well distributed. Sprinkle with the almonds and paprika and let stand for 15 more minutes so the pasta can absorb the flavors.

Serve cold or at room temperature.

EGYPT

MAKES 6 SERVINGS

¼ cup peanut oil

1 teaspoon ground allspice

1 teaspoon ground turmeric

1 teaspoon dried thyme

1 teaspoon salt + ½ teaspoon
salt for the béchamel

1 teaspoon freshly
ground black pepper

½ teaspoon ground cardamom

½ teaspoon ground cinnamon

2 cups chopped onion

1 pound ground lamb

1 cup canned crushed
tomatoes or *passata*

½ cup butter

½ teaspoon ground nutmeg

½ teaspoon ground white pepper

½ cup all-purpose flour

5 cups whole milk

2 eggs, beaten

1 pound dried penne pasta,
cooked for half the time indicated
on the package, rinsed and drained.

Oil or oil spray for the baking dish

Pasta with Béchamel Sauce: *Macarona bel Bechamel*

Sometimes it's possible to tell the origins of a dish from its description. A pasta sauce with pork, tomato, and herbs . . . Italy, right? Soy sauce, fresh ginger, and garlic . . . Chinese? And a rich baked tray of pasta, meat, and dairy . . . That's got to be from someplace in Italy's far north. Except that it isn't. This rich baked dish comes from Egypt. It's hearty enough for the Alps, though, and rich enough for the coldest of days.

1. Put the oil, allspice, turmeric, thyme, salt, black pepper, cardamom, and cinnamon in a large skillet over medium heat and cook and stir until the spices are coated with oil, about 1 minute.

2. Mix in the onions and cook, stirring frequently, until they are translucent and browned at the edges, about 15 minutes.

3. Add the ground lamb and continue to stir frequently until it's well browned, about 15 minutes. Use the back of a wooden spoon to break up big clumps and keep the pieces of meat as small as possible.

4. Mix in the tomato and simmer, stirring occasionally, until the flavors have combined, about 5 minutes. Set aside.

5. Melt the butter in a separate large pan over medium heat and mix in the ½ teaspoon salt, nutmeg, white pepper, and flour and stir continuously until the mixture becomes a thick paste, about 3 minutes.

6. Watch carefully here! In order to get a proper sauce to form, you'll have to use the following technique. Mix in ¼ cup of milk and whisk with the flour paste. When it's fully absorbed, after about 1 minute, add another ¼ cup of milk. After the flour paste has absorbed 1 cup of milk this way, add ½ cup of milk at a time. When you've gotten the flour paste to absorb 3 cups of milk—it should be expanded and gloppy by now—you can add milk 1 cup at a time.

7. When all the milk and flour have combined, slowly whisk in the beaten eggs. If you add the eggs slowly enough and whisk quickly enough, they won't scramble. Remove from the heat and set aside.

8. Preheat the oven to 325 degrees.

9. Combine the cooked pasta with half the finished sauce and toss so that the pasta pieces are evenly coated with the sauce.

10. Oil the bottom of a 4-quart baking dish and cover with half the pasta and sauce mixture. Next, cover that layer with the cooked meat mixture, and then put the rest of the pasta on top. Finally, cover with the remaining béchamel. Bake the assembled tray of pasta, meat, and sauce until the top has browned, about 60 minutes.

Let cool for at least 15 minutes, slice, and serve.

ETHIOPIA

Spiced Spaghetti with Tomato Sauce

With the unmistakable look of classic spaghetti and tomato sauce and the strong fragrance of *berbere* spice, this Ethiopian dish is a real surprise. For a brief while long ago, Ethiopia was an Italian colony. Not much Italian is left there, but spaghetti remains.

1. Put the oil, onion, and garlic in a large pan over medium-low heat and cook, stirring frequently, until the onion turns golden, about 30 minutes.

2. Mix in the *berbere*, tomatoes, salt, and water. Continue to cook uncovered, stirring occasionally, until the mixture has combined and the raw taste is gone, about 20 minutes.

3. Toss with the cooked spaghetti and serve.

MAKES 4 SERVINGS

¼ cup peanut oil

2 cups chopped onion, puréed in a food processor

2 tablespoons crushed and chopped garlic

2 tablespoons *berbere* spice mixture

1½ cups canned crushed tomato or *passata*

1 teaspoon salt

½ cup water

1 pound spaghetti, cooked and drained*

*Macaroni is also used in this dish. And while it's not authentic, ziti or other large pasta shapes hold their own when paired with this sauce.

SOUTH AFRICA

Noodles Boiled in Milk: *Melksnysels*

MAKES 4 SERVINGS

2 cups all-purpose
flour + flour for kneading

¼ teaspoon salt + ¼ teaspoon salt

1 teaspoon baking powder

1 egg

½ cup whole milk + 6 cups
for cooking the noodles

2 tablespoons sugar

2 cinnamon sticks

2 tablespoons butter

When I first heard that South Africans had a traditional noodle dish, I was ready for heat, acidity, and sweetness. I expected something that would go with a big barbecue. Instead, I found *melksnysels,* the most gentle recipe I could ever imagine. It's best thought of as cake braised in sweetened milk.

1. Combine the flour, ¼ teaspoon of salt, baking powder, egg, and ½ cup of milk in a large bowl and mix until you have a stiff dough. I suggest you start with a large wooden spoon and then work the mixture with your hands until the dough forms. If the dough is too soft, add flour, 1 tablespoon at a time, until it firms up. If it's too hard to knead, add milk, 1 tablespoon at a time, until it's kneadable.

2. Sprinkle some flour on a flat surface and knead the dough on it. Knead until a thumb pressed into the mass makes a dent and the dent springs back, about 7 minutes. Then wrap the dough in a kitchen towel or plastic wrap and let rest for about 20 minutes.

3. Use a pasta machine to flatten the dough into a thin sheet. A final setting of 4 will work fine. This dough is really fragile and may need more trips through the machine than most other doughs; just bear with it and it will come out right. Cut the dough into noodles about ½-inch wide and 4 inches long and let them rest on a floured surface.

4. Put the 6 cups of milk, sugar, ¼ tablespoon of salt, and cinnamon sticks in a large pot and bring to a simmer over medium heat. Be careful: if it overheats, it will boil over easily.

5. Put the noodles in the simmering milk and cook, stirring occasionally, until they're tender, about 3 minutes.

6. Use a slotted spoon or strainer with a handle to remove the noodles from the pot. Then put them on serving plates.

7. To serve, ladle some of the sweetened cooking milk over the noodles and top with a pat of butter.

TUNISIA

MAKES 4 SERVINGS

2 tablespoons olive oil

1 pound boneless beef chuck cut into ½-inch cubes

2 cups chopped onion

2 tablespoons crushed and chopped garlic

1 cup canned crushed tomatoes or *passata*

1 teaspoon salt

1 teaspoon ground turmeric

2 tablespoons *harissa* (North African chile paste)

1 teaspoon Spanish paprika

2 bay leaves

3 cups water

1 pound spaghetti, cooked and drained

Tunisian Spaghetti with Meat Sauce

Yet another addition to the spaghetti and meat sauce canon, this time with stewed beef and North African spices. And if you doubt that Tunisians actually eat spaghetti, check with the International Pasta Organization—its statistics tell us that Tunisia is third in the world for pasta consumption per capita. The typical Tunisian eats far more pasta than the average American.

1. Put the oil and beef in a large skillet over high heat and cook, stirring, until the meat is browned—not gray!—about 10 minutes. Remove the meat from the pot and reserve. Do *not* remove the skillet from the heat.

2. Reduce the heat to medium-low and add the onions and garlic. Cook, stirring, until the onions are transparent and the brown bits left by the meat are dissolved into the onion mixture, about 10 minutes.

3. Return the cooked beef to the skillet and add the tomatoes, salt, turmeric, *harissa*, paprika, and bay leaves. Cook, stirring, until the spices have dissolved, then add the water and simmer until the meat becomes very tender and all that remains of the liquid is a thick sauce, about 90 minutes.

4. Serve over spaghetti.

ALBANIA

Baked Spaghetti and Feta: *Pastitsio*

Sometimes you wonder just how simple a food can be. *Pastitsio*, or baked pasta as it's prepared in much of eastern Europe, is normally pretty complicated. Not only is there that pasta, there can be meat, more than one sauce, and multiple cheeses and seasonings. Not in Albania. This is baked pasta in the simplest possible form. So much so that it becomes an entirely different dish. Give it a try. I mean . . . how many Albanian dishes have you made before?

1. Preheat the oven to 325 degrees.

2. Combine the feta, milk, salt, pepper, and eggs in a large bowl and mix well. The eggs should be beaten and fully combined with the milk and feta.

3. Butter a 2-quart baking dish and spread with one-third of the cheese/milk/egg mixture. Then lay three-quarters of the cooked spaghetti in a flat layer over it. Then, cover with the remaining cheese/milk/egg mixture. Finally, spread the remaining spaghetti over it.

4. Bake until the spaghetti on top has browned, about 60 minutes. Let cool 15 minutes before serving.

MAKES 4 SERVINGS

1½ cups crumbled feta cheese

1½ cups whole milk

1 teaspoon salt

1 teaspoon freshly ground pepper

6 eggs

8 ounces spaghetti, cooked, rinsed, and drained

3 tablespoons butter

POLAND

Sweet Noodle Pudding: *Kugel*

This sweet noodle and onion dessert is part of the eastern European Jewish culinary tradition. For many people I know, it's a holiday reminder that there's more to noodles than spaghetti and meat sauce (page 54) or lo mein (page 65). If that's not enough for you, this is one of the very few dishes in this book that can be gratifyingly washed down with a cup of coffee.

1. Melt the butter in a skillet over medium-low heat. Then add the onions and salt, and cook, stirring, until the onions are a deep golden color, about 45 minutes. Remember: When you caramelize onions like this, time is your friend and heat is your enemy. You may have to lower the heat to prevent scorching. Set the onions aside when ready.

2. Preheat the oven to 325 degrees.

3. Combine the farmer cheese with the sour cream, eggs, sugar, brown sugar, cinnamon, cloves, raisins, walnuts, and cooked noodles. Mix well so that all the ingredients are evenly combined.

4. Butter a 9 x 13-inch baking dish, add the noodle mixture, and then bake, covered, until the eggs firm, about 60 minutes. Remove the cover and bake until the noodles on top are well browned, about 30 minutes.

Serve warm with a cup of strong hot tea or coffee.

MAKES 1 KUGEL,
ABOUT 8 SERVINGS

2 tablespoons butter + 2 tablespoons for the baking dish

4 cups sliced red onions

½ teaspoon salt + 1 tablespoon for boiling the noodles

1 cup plain farmer cheese (about one 7⅟ ounce package)

2 cups sour cream

4 beaten eggs

½ cup sugar

½ cup light brown sugar

1 teaspoon ground cinnamon

½ teaspoon ground cloves

1 cup raisins

1 cup chopped walnuts

1 pound egg noodles, cooked and drained

THEY'RE NOT PORK AND THEY'RE NOT SHELLFISH: SO, ARE NOODLES KOSHER?

MOST OF US KNOW THE BASICS: no pork, no shellfish, no cheeseburgers. And if you visit kosher homes on a regular basis, you'll have experienced far more. Kosher laws, or kashrut, are part of basic Judaism. Following them properly helps create the structure for an observant Jewish home life. If you keep a kosher home, you'll understand the issues at hand here in a profound and personal way. The rest of us need to study up a bit for the times we're either invited over or hosting observant guests.

The baseline rules are spelled out in the Old Testament. And in the ensuing thousands of years, Jewish scholars have analyzed, refined, and clarified them. For the purposes of this book, it's enough to know that permitted foods are divided into three groups: meat, dairy, and neutral. Meat and dairy must be kept separate; hence the banning of cheeseburgers. This is true for all other dishes too. For a plate of spaghetti and meat sauce to be kosher, not only would its ingredients have to be kosher, it would also have to have absolutely no dairy products in it. Just meat and "neutral" ingredients.

In theory, eggs are neutral, but in practice, it's much more complicated. To be kosher, eggs have to come from kosher chickens and be free of blood spots. This means checking each egg for blood spots after it has been cracked open and before it's added to the dough. In addition, eggs from a kosher chicken lose their kosher status if the chicken dies by natural causes before the eggs are consumed.

During the holiday of Passover, things get trickier. An important part of the holiday is the avoidance of leavened grain. And it's this process of leavening, the way wheat expands and becomes pliable when wet, that makes noodles made from wheat flour tender and, well . . . delicious. Experts may debate the correctness of noodles made from other grains like rice flour or potato starch, and I will leave the debate to them. My suggestion? Put noodles aside for Passover and make something else.

The rest of the year, noodles made with kosher eggs can be served alongside anything, but you might want to be extra-safe and leave the eggs out. Noodles made from the basic dried noodles recipe on page 21 using durum semolina flour will do the job well. If you must have more richness, substitute ½ cup olive oil for half of the water when you're mixing the dough. This will make your noodles vegan too, not a bad combination.

HUNGARY

Sautéed Cabbage and Noodles: *Haluska*

Ah! Noodles and shredded cabbage together in a pan; obviously Chinese, right? Nope. It's Hungarian and features sour cream, something that never made it into anybody's wok.

1. Put the butter, onions, salt, and pepper in a large skillet and cook, stirring frequently, over medium-low heat until the onions turn translucent and begin to brown at the edges, about 20 minutes.

2. Mix in the cabbage and cook with occasional stirring until it's tender, about 20 minutes.

3. Remove from the heat and immediately mix in the cooked noodles and the sour cream. Toss until the cream covers the noodles and cabbage evenly.

Serve right away.

MAKES 4 SERVINGS

2 tablespoons butter

2 cups sliced onions

1 teaspoon salt

1 teaspoon freshly ground pepper

5 cups shredded cabbage

1 recipe egg noodles cut into ½ x 3-inch strips, or 1 package (about 12 ounces) broad egg noodles, cooked, rinsed, and drained

1 cup sour cream

MAKES 4 SERVINGS

¼ cup butter

1 cup coarsely crushed walnuts

3 tablespoons sugar

½ teaspoon ground cinnamon

1 tablespoon lemon zest

½ recipe egg noodles (page 23) cut in ½ x 3-inch strips, or 8 ounces broad egg noodles, cooked and drained in either case

Noodles with Walnuts: *Dios Metelt*

Most Americans would never think of putting noodles and walnuts together. That doesn't mean that other people wouldn't. In Turkey, noodles and walnuts are combined with arugula (page 220 to make a savory dish; in Hungary, a bit of cinnamon and sugar is added to make this sweet dessert.

1. Melt the butter in a saucepan over medium-low heat and add the walnuts, sugar, cinnamon, and lemon zest. Cook and stir until the sugar has dissolved in the butter and coated the walnuts.

2. Put the cooked noodles in a large bowl and toss with the butter and nut mixture.

Serve right away. It's supposed to be warm.

GREECE

MAKES 4 SERVINGS

1 tablespoon olive oil

1 teaspoon salt

1 teaspoon freshly ground pepper

½ teaspoon ground cinnamon

½ teaspoon ground allspice

½ teaspoon ground cloves

1 pound ground lamb

2 cups chopped onions

3 tablespoons crushed
and chopped fresh garlic

1 cup red wine

2 cups canned crushed tomatoes

1 pound spaghetti,
cooked and drained

Greek-Style Spaghetti with Meat Sauce: *Makaronia me Kima*

Well, here we are again in that vast world of spaghetti with meat sauce. This time we're in Greece, where the spices are different, the meat is lamb, and there's a unique way of browning the meat and onions together. It's the same, but different.

1. Put the olive oil, salt, pepper, cinnamon, allspice, and cloves in a large skillet over medium heat and cook, stirring, until the spices are fragrant and coated with oil, about 3 minutes.

2. Add the lamb, onions, and garlic and cook, stirring occasionally until the onions are translucent and the meat has browned, about 20 minutes.

3. Mix in the red wine and tomatoes and cook, stirring occasionally, until the raw taste is gone and about a quarter of the liquid has evaporated, about 30 minutes.

4. Remove from the heat and serve over the cooked spaghetti.

IMMIGRATION: THE MODERN SILK ROAD

IF YOU TAKE A LOOK at how foods spread a thousand years ago, there was an obvious vector—the Silk Road. The trade route from Venice to Beijing transported spices, recipes, and even livestock. Both noodles and dumplings were carried by Silk Road traders, as were sheep and chickens. Today, the Silk Road has been replaced by container ships, airliners, and railroads, and when foods jump from one culture to another, they're propelled by immigration. It's a bit more scattershot, but the results are even more interesting. If you want material proof, head into a local Chinese restaurant. Although Chinese American is by no means the only global adaptation of the Emperor's cuisine, the sheer number of Chinese restaurants in the United States tells a story in itself.

Chinese dishes morphed as they spread around the world; it's something you can see clearly in this book. Our own chicken lo mein (recipe page 65) is a close cousin to Filipino *pancit bihon* (page 139), Singaporean fried curry noodles (page 169), and Nepali *chow chow* (page 189). All of these dishes began when Chinese expats started cooking with a mixture of local and traditional ingredients, and all are favorites today in their adopted countries.

If you tried to be a purist about these things, you could argue that all noodle dishes had their origins in either China or Italy—indeed, that seems right to our modern American sensibilities. Yet if you take one step further back, you're on that Silk Road without any real way to pinpoint exactly where people started making noodles in the first place.

India, too, has a vast number of Chinese restaurants, and they serve dishes that only faintly resemble Chinese American or actual Chinese. I always thought that hakka noodles (page 196) were the limit of noodle penetration in India—that is, until I started researching the recipe for *sevai* (page 199). The package the dry noodles came in had a sort of pop Chinese motif with dragons in yellow and red. Indeed, it seemed like this dish was seen as Chinese by Indian diners even though the recipe and ingredients list appears relentlessly Indian in our eyes.

Italian noodles didn't exactly have the same vector as Chinese. Yes, Italians did move all over the world and open restaurants, but they weren't the only ones serving Italian food. Almost from the first moment it was introduced, spaghetti was hugely popular in the United States. And we Americans did as much to spread the food as Italians themselves, as evidenced by the Philippine dish spaghetti with sliced hot dogs (page 140).

Spaghetti seems to have another reason for its wide proliferation—it travels well, due to its light weight and resistance to spoilage. It can be brought to an edible state long after rice or beans have gone stale, and—as the recipes in this book demonstrate—can be adapted to almost any cuisine.

It would be easy to leave this whole thing at the feet of hardworking immigrants fanning out across the globe in an effort to build better lives. The problem with that is that we would be ignoring food history's ugly uncle, imperialism; that is, the economic and military occupation of one country by another. Imperialism is why you see spaghetti and meat sauce in so many cultures. No, it wasn't the marauding Italians—although they did occupy Ethiopia and brought forth a great dish (page 229). Instead, it was American soldiers that brought spaghetti and macaroni with them wherever they went, and hot dogs, too.

From our perspective, it's almost impossible to tell which foods will become new immigrant classics, which will be subsumed into that vast pool of "American" dishes, and which will be forgotten about before next Christmas. You just never know.

BELGIUM

Beer-Braised Beef over Noodles: *Carbonnade de Boeuf*

MAKES 4 SERVINGS

Those Belgians know their food! What could be a better combination than beef, beer, and noodles? With the meat braising and a big pot of water boiling for the noodles, you can easily imagine a group of Belgian monks whipping up a batch on a damp winter night.

1. Put the lard in a pot over medium heat and add the thyme, salt, and pepper. Cook, stirring, until the seasonings are coated with the fat.

2. Add the beef and cook, stirring frequently, until the meat is well browned on all sides, about 15 minutes. Remove from the pot and set aside, leaving the pot on the heat (don't clean it!).

3. Add the onions and bay leaves to the pot and cook, stirring frequently, until they're tender, golden, and have absorbed the brown bits of beef stuck to the pan, about 15 minutes.

4. Mix in the cooked beef and beer, lower the heat to medium-low, and simmer, covered, stirring occasionally, until the meat is very tender, about 90 minutes. Note that the meat will become very tough before it starts tenderizing, after about 60 minutes.
To serve, arrange the noodles in a thin layer on a serving platter and cover with the meat and gravy. A touch of hot mustard on the side makes a good accompaniment.

¼ cup lard or beef suet

2 teaspoons dried thyme

1 teaspoon salt

1 teaspoon freshly ground pepper

2 pounds boneless beef chuck cut into 1-inch cubes

2 cups thinly sliced onions

2 bay leaves

2 cups Belgian-style ale (make sure you measure liquid and not foam)

1 recipe basic egg noodles, cut into ½-inch wide strips, cooked and drained

Hot mustard for serving (optional)

SPAIN

Spanish Pasta with Seafood: *Fideuà*

MAKES 4 SERVINGS

Does this dish look familiar to you? It should—it's the noodle version of paella, the dish that screams "Spain!" in restaurants around the world. Why paella gets all the glory is a question for another time. Give this dish a try instead.

1. Put the olive oil in a wok or skillet over high heat and add the pasta. Cook, stirring, until the pasta begins to brown, about 3 minutes.

2. Reduce the heat to medium and mix in the garlic, saffron, paprika, salt, and pepper. Stir until all the spices and noodles are mixed well, about 1 minute.

3. Mix in the monkfish and tomatoes and cook, stirring, until the fish appears opaque and the tomato looses its raw flavor, about 5 minutes.

4. Mix in the shrimp, scallops, and mussels and cook, stirring occasionally, until the shrimp is cooked and the noodles are tender, about 10 minutes. If the pan dries out, add water, 1 cup at a time, until it's moist enough to tenderize the noodles.

Serve right away.

½ cup olive oil

½ pound angel hair pasta, broken into 2- to 3-inch lengths

2 tablespoons crushed and chopped garlic

½ teaspoon saffron threads

1 teaspoon Spanish paprika

1 teaspoon salt

1 teaspoon freshly ground pepper

½ pound monkfish fillet cut into ½-inch cubes

1 cup canned, crushed tomatoes

½ pound peeled shrimp

½ pound scallops

1 pound mussels

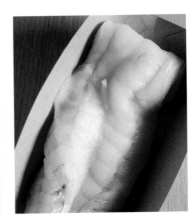

MAKES 4 SERVINGS

¼ cup olive oil

1 teaspoon salt

1 teaspoon freshly ground
black pepper

2 cups chopped onion

3 tablespoons crushed
and chopped garlic

1 pound fresh mild
chorizo sausage, sliced

2 cups chopped green bell peppers

3 cups canned crushed tomatoes

1 pound penne pasta,
cooked and drained

Penne with Sausage and Peppers: *Macarrones a la Española*

Pasta with tomato sauce may have started in Italy, but it's adaptable enough to have become a favorite food in many cultures. Here's one way they do it in Spain.

1. Put the oil, salt, and pepper in a skillet over medium heat and mix in the onions and garlic. Cook, stirring frequently, until the onions are tender and the garlic starts to brown at the edges, about 15 minutes.

2. Add the chorizo and bell peppers and cook, stirring frequently, until the sausage starts to brown at the edges and the peppers become tender, about 15 minutes.

3. Mix in the tomatoes, reduce the heat to medium-low, and simmer, stirring occasionally, until the flavors combine, about 20 minutes.

4. Toss with the cooked penne pasta and serve right away.

2 tablespoons olive oil

2 tablespoons lard

2 tablespoons butter

1 teaspoon salt

1 teaspoon freshly ground pepper

½ cup pine nuts

3 tablespoons crushed
and chopped garlic

½ pound boneless pork stew
meat cut into ½-inch cubes

1 cup chopped ham

1 cup coarsely chopped
chicken gizzards

1 cup canned chopped tomatoes

2 cups red wine

2 tablespoons chopped parsley

6 cups water

12 ounces *fideos*—fine
Spanish noodles, dry

1 cup chopped chicken livers

Catalan-Style Noodles: *Tallarines a la Catalana*

Why is it that we always speak of Spain as being sunny and hot and yet its noodle dishes all seem to be hearty stews better suited to snowy winters than sunny coastlines? This recipe is no exception. For a start, it features pork as well as chicken livers, which are stewed in red wine. Delicious and classic, but something you'd want to eat after a day in the mountains, not a day on the beach.

1. Put the oil, lard, butter, salt, and pepper in a large pot over medium heat and stir until the butter melts, about 1 minute.

2. Mix in the pine nuts, garlic, pork, ham, and chicken gizzards and cook, stirring frequently, until the pork has browned, about 20 minutes.

3. Add the tomatoes, red wine, parsley, and water and cook uncovered, stirring occasionally, until the pork and gizzards are tender, about 60 minutes.

4. Mix in the *fideos* and simmer until they start to become tender, about 5 minutes. If there isn't enough liquid to soak them, add water, 1 cup at a time, until you have enough to cover the ingredients.

5. Mix in the chicken livers and cook, stirring occasionally, until they're barely cooked and the noodles are completely tender, about 5 minutes.

Serve hot and right away. This dish looks like it can be made ahead and reheated, but its ingredients conspire against it; the noodles will turn to mush and the chicken offal to rubber.

ANDORRA

Ham, Bean, and Noodle Stew: *Escudella*

⤳

There are countries a thousand times larger than Andorra that nobody knows anything about. We all know one thing about Andorra, though: it's really small. Well, now you know something else—its national dish is a ham, bean, and noodle stew called *escudella*. Actually, Andorra is pretty close to the Catalan region of Spain and their cuisines are similar. You might even find a bowl of *escudella* in Barcelona.

1. Check the navy beans for stones or other debris, then rinse them off, soak them overnight, and rinse them once more. Set aside.

2. Put the pork bones, oxtail, and 4 quarts of water (16 cups) in a large pot over high heat. Bring to a boil for 1 minute, reduce the heat to low, and simmer, covered, stirring occasionally, until the meat easily comes off the bones, about 3 hours. If foam forms on the surface of the liquid, skim it off. Remove the bones and scrape off any remaining meat. Discard the bones and return the meat to the liquid.

3. Mix in the soaked beans, rice, chicken, and ham and sausage meat, and simmer, covered, stirring occasionally, until the chicken is cooked through and the rice grains have burst, about 60 minutes.

4. Mix in the potato, leeks, and cabbage and simmer, covered, stirring occasionally, until the potato is tender, about 30 minutes.

MAKES 6 SERVINGS

1 cup dried navy beans

2 pounds ham or smoked pork bones (a smoked ham hock is perfect here)

1½ pounds oxtail

¼ cup rice

1 pound bone-in chicken parts (thighs work well here)

1 pound ham steak, cut in ½-inch pieces

1 pound mild Italian sausage meat, formed into 6 large balls

1 cup peeled, chopped potato

1 cup sliced leeks

2 cups chopped savoy cabbage

2 teaspoons salt

1 pound large pasta shells, cooked and drained

5. Taste the broth. If it needs it—and only if it needs it (the ham and ham/pork bones may lend sufficient flavor)—add the salt. If you're not sure, add a tiny bit of salt at a time, mix it in well, and taste it again until it's right.

6. To assemble the dish, put a layer of cooked shells in the bottom of a serving bowl and spoon the ham and bean mixture over it. Make sure everybody gets a meatball and some chicken too.

PROFESSOR OF BONEOLOGY

HAVING MADE, WITH MIXED RESULTS, more than a few batches of broth, I decided it might be time to talk to an expert. Bob del Grosso is a culinary instructor, butcher on an organic farm, and artisan meat curer. He spoke with me as he butchered a whole calf, stopping only to make coffee or stir the big stockpot on the stove in one corner of the butchering room.

Bob wasn't impressed with my modest broth-making experiences, especially when I expounded on how bones give soup its soul. And then I made myself sound worse, belittling concentrates, boxed broths, and anything flavored with MSG. I was a dilettante if there ever was one.

The professor began his lesson by shaking his head. "Nothing wrong with MSG," he told me. "It has sodium, so it adds salt and flavor." So why then was he here in this remote (by northeastern US standards, anyway) farm, cutting up a calf while a pot of chicken stock simmered ten feet away?

"There's stock and then there's *stock*," he said, showing me the calf's femur and some shinbone. Big bones with lots of cartilage, just what you need for real substance. I kept thinking about how much of the broth I sampled just tasted like flavored water. "Water is essential for breaking down connective tissue," he explained, and by adding bones with lots of connective tissue you can get a liquid with real structure. For chicken, the method isn't so different; instead of adding big bones, you put in extra feet and/or skin; parts of the bird loaded with gelatin, to get the same effect.

I did notice that Bob's chicken stock was made with wings and necks rather than feet, but it didn't take much effort to see that his was more than meat-flavored water. When he scooped up some with a ladle, it had viscosity. It gracefully returned to the pot with none of the splashing of mere H$_2$O.

I don't know what I was expecting, but Bob's stock-making instructions proved something of a letdown. "Roast the bones if you want a dark stock or just wash them in cold water for a lighter one," he said. Then just simmer them for as long as you can. He pointed to his simmer—there were just a few bubbles breaking the surface of the liquid. And that was it. No magic ingredient. The way to do it is to do it. The magic comes from the time and care with which you simmer the bones, not from anything special you do while they're cooking.

PORTUGAL

Sweet Noodle Pudding: *Aletria*

How many noodle desserts do you know? This one is a Portuguese Christmas specialty that tastes an awful lot like English rice pudding.

1. Put the milk, lemon zest, and cinnamon stick in a large pot and bring to a boil over high heat. Stir frequently to make sure it doesn't boil over.

2. When it boils for 1 minute, reduce the heat to medium-low, mix in the sugar, brown sugar, and salt and cook uncovered, stirring frequently, until a third of the liquid has evaporated, about 40 minutes. Then remove and discard the cinnamon stick.

3. Mix in the butter and pasta and cook, stirring frequently, until the pasta is tender, about 3 minutes.

4. Remove one cup of the cooking liquid and put it in a bowl. Then add the egg yolks to the liquid, one drop at a time with vigorous whisking until the yolks are completely combined. If the yolk hardens, you're adding it too quickly; take a deep breath and slow down.

5. Slowly mix the yolk mixture back into the simmering milk and noodle liquid. When they're mixed thoroughly, pour into a serving bowl.

Let the pudding cool and firm up for at least 15 minutes before serving.

MAKES 6 SERVINGS

2 quarts whole milk

¼ cup finely chopped lemon zest

1 cinnamon stick

½ cup white sugar

½ cup dark brown sugar

¼ teaspoon salt

½ cup butter

1 pound *fideos* or *filini* pasta, or angel hair pasta broken into 2-inch pieces

4 egg yolks, whisked together

MEXICO

Noodle Casserole: *Sopa Seca*

Even if your Spanish is as bad as mine, you may notice that the name of this dish translates into English as "dry soup." Not only is this dish not a soup, it turns regular pasta into an ingredient that's somewhere between instant noodles (page 98) and pretzel sticks, ready to absorb this amazing sauce.

1. Put the onion, garlic, tomato, chipotle peppers, cilantro, salt, and pepper in a food processor and pulse until the ingredients are liquefied, about 2 minutes.

2. Pour the liquid into a large pot, add the chicken broth, put it on medium-low heat, and simmer, stirring occasionally, until a quarter of the liquid has evaporated, about 30 minutes.

3. While the seasoning liquid is simmering, put the cup of oil in a small skillet over high heat. When it's hot—a thermometer should read at least 325 degrees—add 1 bunch of the *fideos* and fry until they're golden brown, about 30 seconds. Remove them from the oil with a slotted spoon, and drain on paper towels. Repeat this process until all the noodles are cooked.

4. Combine the fried noodles with the simmering onion/tomato/chipotle liquid. Stir until the noodles are evenly coated in sauce. Then cook, stirring occasionally, until the noodles start to become tender, about 10 minutes.

MAKES 4 SERVINGS

1 cup chopped onion

2 tablespoons chopped fresh garlic

2 cups canned peeled tomatoes

3 canned chipotle peppers + 1 tablespoon sauce from the can

¼ cup fresh cilantro

1 teaspoon salt

½ teaspoon freshly ground pepper

2 cups chicken broth

1 cup peanut oil

12 ounces *fideos,* the thin Spanish noodles

½ cup crumbled Mexican white cheese (or substitute chopped Colby cheese)

½ cup sour cream

5. Mix in the cheese and toss a few times to make sure the pieces are evenly distributed.

6. Transfer the noodles and sauce onto serving plates and top with the sour cream.

Serve right away.

Cowboy Beef and Noodle Stew: *Puchero Vaquero*

Stews are a branch of Mexican cuisine that seems lost on most Americans. This one is as simple as they get—meat, vegetables, rice, and noodles.

1. Bring the 6 cups of water to a boil in a large pot and add the beef, salt, and achiote. Reduce the heat to medium-low and cook, stirring occasionally, until the meat starts to become tender and the achiote is fully dissolved, about 1 hour. Check the pot occasionally and skim off any scum that forms on the surface as necessary.

2. Mix in the rice and continue cooking, stirring occasionally, until it becomes tender, about 15 minutes.

3. Mix in the zucchini and chayote and continue cooking with occasional stirring until they become tender, about 20 minutes.

4. Mix in the spinach and *fideos* and cook until the noodles are tender, about 5 minutes (give the noodles an occasional stir with a fork to prevent the noodles from clumping together).

5. To serve, ladle the stew into bowls and sprinkle with the cilantro, onion, and hot red peppers. Put a lime wedge at the side of each bowl as a finishing touch.

MAKES 4 SERVINGS

6 cups water

1½ pounds beef chuck, cut into 1-inch cubes

2 teaspoons salt

1 tablespoon achiote paste (also called annatto)

¼ cup long-grain white rice

1 cup chopped zucchini

1 cup chopped chayote

2 cups chopped spinach, or one 10-ounce package frozen

6 ounces *fideos*, the thin Spanish noodles

¼ cup chopped cilantro leaves

½ cup chopped red onion

¼ cup *ají picante*, hot red pickled peppers

1 lime, cut in quarters

MAKES 4 SERVINGS

Oil cooking spray

8 cups fresh plum tomato
wedges (about 3 pounds)

2 teaspoons salt + ½ teaspoon
for final seasoning

1 teaspoon freshly ground pepper

1 cup chopped onion

2 tablespoons crushed
and chopped garlic

3 tablespoons peanut oil

2 cups chicken broth

2 cups water

6 ounces *fideos**

*Mexican grocery stores typically
sell them in packages of this size.

Tomato Noodle Soup: *Sopa de fideos*

How can tomato soup with noodles be Mexican? Well, leaving aside the fact that tomatoes were eaten in Mexico long before they were grown in Europe, this dish uses classic Mexican technique: first roasting, then blending the tomatoes, and finally cooking the purée to make a soup. A bit of Mexico in a bowl.

1. Preheat the oven to 425 degrees.

2. Spray a baking sheet with oil and spread the tomato wedges out on the baking sheet, sprinkling the wedges with the salt and pepper. Spray the tomatoes with oil and bake until the skins start to brown, about 45 minutes. Remove from the oven and allow to cool.

3. Put the cooked tomatoes, onion, and garlic in a blender and liquify. There should be nothing solid left. This requires several minutes of pulsing.

4. Put the oil in a large skillet over medium-low heat and mix in the tomato and onion mixture. Cook, stirring frequently, until the bitter flavor is gone, about 30 minutes.

5. Add the chicken broth and the 2 cups of water, raise the heat to high, and let the liquid come to a boil. Then mix in the *fideos*, reduce the heat to medium-low, and simmer covered, stirring occasionally, until the noodles are tender, about 8 minutes.

6. Taste the soup; if it needs salt—this depends entirely on the kind of broth you use—add it ½ teaspoon at a time, until it's right. Be careful here—there's no way to take salt out once it's in there.

Serve right away.

BRAZIL

Brazilian Spaghetti and Tuna Salad: *Macarrão com Atum*

MAKES 2 SERVINGS

Is any person—or, for that matter, any other ingredient—as well traveled as spaghetti? No other dish has seen more variations on more continents. This one, a Brazilian version of tuna salad, takes those long strings of noodle in yet another direction.

1. Combine the tuna, mayonnaise, olives, egg, parsley, lemon juice, salt, and pepper and mix well. Make sure all the ingredients are well distributed.

2. To assemble, toss the spaghetti with the tuna mixture until the pasta is evenly coated.

Serve at room temperature or chilled.

1 can (about 5½ ounces) solid white tuna packed in water, drained

½ cup mayonnaise

1 cup chopped pitted olives

1 boiled egg, chopped

1 tablespoon chopped parsley

1 tablespoon lemon juice

1 teaspoon salt

½ teaspoon ground white pepper

8 ounces spaghetti, cooked, rinsed, and drained

MAKES 4 SERVINGS

3 tablespoons unsalted butter

3 tablespoons crushed
and chopped fresh garlic

1 pound boneless chicken breasts or
thighs, cut into ½-inch-wide strips

1 teaspoon salt

1 teaspoon freshly ground pepper

2 cups drained, canned
peeled tomatoes, coarsely chopped

¼ cup chopped pitted green olives

1½ cups (about 1 can) hearts
of palm, cut into ¼-inch lengths

1 pound spaghetti or
linguine, cooked and drained

3 tablespoons chopped chives

Spaghetti with Chicken and Hearts of Palm: *Macarrão com molho de frango e palmito*

Even though there are a hundred recipes in this book, I'm pretty sure this is the only one that has a tree trunk as a key ingredient. That's the way noodles are. They can be adapted to anything. This recipe takes two global ingredients—noodles and chicken—and combines them with the very Latin American heart of palm.

1. Melt the butter in a large skillet over medium heat and add the garlic. Cook, stirring, until the garlic starts to brown at the edges, about 3 minutes.

2. Add the chicken, salt, and pepper and stir frequently until the chicken appears cooked on the outside, about 5 minutes.

3. Mix in the tomatoes, olives, and hearts of palm and cook, stirring occasionally, until the tomatoes have lost their raw flavor, the chicken is completely cooked, and the garlic is very tender, about 10 minutes.

4. Toss with the cooked pasta and chives and serve right away.

AROUND THE WORLD WITH A BOX OF SPAGHETTI

WHAT IS THIS THING CALLED spaghetti that travels to every corner of the world? Why is it so often accompanied by its longtime companion, tomatoes? Spaghetti has a way of getting around. From its birthplace in Italy, it's wound up in America as spaghetti and meat sauce (page 54), the Philippines, with slices of hot dog (page 140), and in Ethiopia, with tomato sauce and local *berbere* spices. The flavors of the newly adopted host country are obvious against the backdrop of cooked dried pasta.

Easy to manufacture, easy to store, and easy to cook, spaghetti has found its way into an astounding array of world cuisines. Unlike steak or sushi, it doesn't symbolize wealth. Spaghetti is just there. Buy it for pennies, open the box, boil it up, and make it your own.

The range of nations that have done just that is pretty much a list of all nations. Dishes that didn't even make it into this book include Swedish spaghetti with melted cheese, Mexican with chiles and a kaleidoscope of herbs, Taiwanese with pork and brown sauce, or Argentinian with corned beef—all are riffs that utilize pasta as a vehicle for whatever ingredient is prized by the locals.

And that poor old basic Italian tomato sauce? You can find that on spaghetti in almost every corner of the world too.

PERU

Chicken and Noodle Soup: *Caldo de Gallina*

Not only can a book be filled with noodle recipes, volumes could be written on the subject of chicken noodle soup. This version is from Peru, a country known both for its soups and its unique take on otherwise typical dishes. For the record, Peru has a long tradition of borrowing ingredients and methods from Asia. It's no coincidence that a bowl of *caldo de gallina* resembles a bowl of Asian noodle soup.

1. Put the water in a large pot over high heat and add the chicken, salt, and pepper. Cook, stirring occasionally, until the liquid comes to a boil. Let it boil for 1 minute, then reduce the heat to medium-low and simmer, covered, continuing to stir occasionally until the chicken is cooked through, about 30 minutes.

2. Mix in the potatoes and continue to simmer until they're tender, about 30 minutes.

3. Add the scallion greens and cook until tender, about 2 minutes.

4. Assemble the soup as if it were an Asian noodle soup. First put the cooked noodles at the bottom of the bowl, then ladle the liquid/potato mixture over it. And finally, top with the cooked chicken pieces and egg.

Serve piping hot and right away.

MAKES 2 SERVINGS

6 cups water

1 pound bone-in chicken parts (legs or thighs are ideal)

1 teaspoon salt

1 teaspoon freshly ground black pepper

1 cup potato, peeled and cut in large chunks

½ cup scallion greens, cut into ½-inch pieces

8 ounces dry linguine or fettuccine pasta, cooked, rinsed, and drained

2 hard-cooked eggs, cut in half lengthwise

MAKES 4 SERVINGS

2 tablespoons peanut
oil + ½ cup peanut oil

1 cup chopped onions

2 tablespoons crushed
and chopped fresh garlic

1 teaspoon salt

1 teaspoon freshly ground pepper

2 cups fresh basil leaves

3 cups fresh spinach leaves

¼ cup chopped walnuts

1 cup crumbled *queso blanco**

1 pound spaghetti or
linguine, cooked and drained

*A firm white Latin American
cheese. Substitute Colby
cheese, chopped into dice-sized
pieces, if you're unable to find it.

Pasta with Green Sauce: *Tallarines Verdes*

When food tells us a story, it can be of love, terrain, or history, and if we're lucky, all three. That's the case with this dish from Peru. More than anything, it's an homage to pesto, the traditional bright green sauce from Liguria, Italy (page 117). It shows how a dish that's grounded in the soil and climate of one place can transition into something a bit different on the other side of the world.

1. Put the 2 tablespoons of peanut oil, onions, garlic, salt, and pepper in a skillet over medium heat. Cook and stir until the onions are translucent, about 10 minutes.

2. Add the basil and spinach leaves and cook, stirring, until they just wilt, about 3 minutes. Remove from the heat.

3. Put the ½ cup of peanut oil, cooked vegetables, walnuts, and *queso blanco* in a blender and purée. I find that pulsing the blender 10 or 20 times gives the best result. It's okay for it to be grainy, but there shouldn't be any big chunks.

4. Toss with the just-cooked-and-still-hot pasta.

THE SOUTH AMERICAN PASTA PARADOX: VENEZUELA VERSUS PERU

No less a group than the International Pasta Organization tells us that, per capita, Venezuela is second only to Italy in pasta consumption. This would make you think that the country is filled with all sorts of fascinating noodle recipes. Yet anybody who spends quality time with Venezuela's menus and cookbooks will quickly see that noodle cookery there seems to devote itself to authentic reproductions of Italian dishes. Checking out the Venezuelan version of lasagna, you find béchemel sauce, a key ingredient in the boot-shaped-country's offering that seems to disappear when the dish is cooked elsewhere. Yet Peru, a nation with much lower pasta consumption, has a whole host of noodle dishes that reflect that country and its culture.

Go figure.

CHILE

Beef and Egg Soup with Fresh Pasta: *Pancutras*

South America is big on meal-sized soups like this one from Chile. What they all have in common is the amount of work that goes into making them. A South American soup is what some people I know call "a project," and *pancutras* is a project and a cooking school rolled into one. Make the broth from scratch and learn about bones and stock, make the noodles and learn some dough-making technique. Assemble it all and it's yours—a great meal in a bowl.

1. Preheat the oven to 425 degrees.

2. Coat a baking sheet with olive oil spray, put the beef bones on it, season the bones with the salt and pepper, give them another spray of oil, and bake until they're well browned, about 45 minutes. Remove from the oven and set aside.

3. Put the roasted bones, onion quarters, and cloves in a large pot along with the 6 quarts of water. Bring it to a boil over high heat and let it boil for 1 minute. Then reduce the heat to medium-low and simmer, covered, stirring occasionally until the bits of meat have fallen off the bones and the onions have become very tender, about 1 hour. (Skim off any white foam that forms on the surface.) Then reduce the heat to low and continue to simmer uncovered until the onions dissolve, about 2 more hours. Remove the bones, scrape any extra meat off them, return the meat to the pot, and discard the bones. Reserve this liquid. This is the broth, your liquid gold.

Olive oil cooking spray

5 pounds beef soup bones

1 teaspoon salt + 2 teaspoons for the finished soup

1 teaspoon freshly ground pepper + 1 teaspoon for the finished soup

2 whole onions, peeled and quartered + 2 cups sliced onions

6 whole cloves

6 quarts water + ½ cup for the dough

2 cups all-purpose flour

¼ cup olive oil + 2 tablespoons olive oil for sautéing the onions

3 tablespoons crushed and chopped fresh garlic

1 pound ground beef

2 cups peeled and chopped yellow potatoes

1 cup sliced carrot

4 eggs, broken into a bowl and scrambled a bit

1 cup green peas (frozen are okay)

¼ cup chopped parsley

4. While the beef broth is simmering, make the noodles by combining the flour, olive oil, and ½ cup of water in a large bowl and mix with a wooden spoon until a dough forms. It should be about the same texture as Play-Doh and easy to knead. If it's too wet, add flour, 1 tablespoon at a time, until it's right. If it's too dry, add water, again, 1 tablespoon at a time, until it's right.

5. Scatter some flour on a flat surface and knead the dough until it becomes elastic, about 5 minutes. Then wrap it in plastic or cloth and let it rest for 30 minutes or so.

6. Scatter a bit more flour on a flat surface and roll the dough out into a sheet. If you have a pasta machine, use thickness setting 4. Then cut the dough into 1½ x 1½-inch squares and let them dry a bit on a sheet of parchment paper while you continue cooking.

7. Put the olive oil in a large pot over medium heat and mix in the sliced onions and garlic and cook, stirring frequently, until the onions have become translucent, about 15 minutes.

8. Mix in the ground beef and keep cooking, stirring frequently until the beef is well browned, about 15 minutes. Use a wooden spoon to break the meat up into the smallest pieces possible.

9. Add the beef broth (you should have at least 3 quarts), potato, carrot, and salt and pepper. Reduce the heat to medium-low and

simmer uncovered until the potato is tender and the liquid has reduced by a quarter, about 40 minutes.

10. Increase the heat to high and bring the soup to a boil. When the liquid is boiling, give it a stir and add the eggs. Wait 1 full minute and then reduce the heat back to medium-low. Stir it a bit to separate the eggs into large pieces.

11. Mix in the noodles, peas, and parsley and stir until the noodles are cooked, about 3 minutes.

Serve hot.

APPENDIX: FINDING AND SELECTING INGREDIENTS

Most of the ingredients called for in this book are pretty easy to find. Some are in supermarkets, and many others are in ethnic groceries or bulk food shops. The more unusual ones might take a bit more effort to locate. This list includes some tips on where to look, and what to look for.

Achiote paste—Also called annatto. Looks like brick-red clay. Find it in Latin American grocery stores.

Anchovy fillets—Even though they cost a bit more, try to find the ones packed in olive oil and sold in glass jars.

Asafoetida—Also known as *hing;* make sure you buy the powdered form in a resealable package—it's strong stuff.

Beef broth—If you're not making it yourself, try a few different brands to see which one you like best. Many people swear by the boxed varieties, although I've had pastes I like too. Save the dry cubes for camping trips.

Beef jerky—The American term for strips of dried beef. Make sure that the jerky you use has no other seasoning than the salt that's required to dry it.

Belacan— Malaysian fermented shrimp paste. Larger Asian markets usually stock it in the Malaysian section; otherwise, look for it among other pastes and concentrates.

Belgian-style ale—Many American microbreweries offer a version of this. Don't forget to buy some to drink alongside your meal too.

Berbere spice mixture—An Ethiopian specialty, it can be found at Ethiopian grocery markets and specialty spice shops.

Black cumin seeds—Also called nigella seeds, but easiest to find as *kalonji,* or onion seeds; find them at Indian grocery stores.

Bonito flakes, dried—The shaved fish of Yoko Ono fame. Find them in the Japanese section of Asian grocery stores and supermarkets or at Japanese specialty stores.

Borlotti beans—An Italian specialty. If you can't find them, substitute the very similar cranberry bean.

Bottarga (dried mullet roe)—Again, an Italian specialty; called "Italian caviar" by some. Like Parmesan, it's sold as either solid blocks you grate yourself or pregrated. Can be ordered online.

Capers—It doesn't matter if you buy salted or brined. They're used the same way.
Chayote—This is technically a fruit but it's eaten like a vegetable; it looks a bit like a green pear. Both Latin and Asian markets will have it.

Chicken broth—As with beef, if you're not making it yourself, try a few different brands to see which one you like best. Many people prefer the boxes over the cans, although I've had pastes I like too. Best to save the dry cubes for camping trips.

Chile oil—Supermarkets with good Asian sections sometimes carry it; otherwise, you'll need to visit a Chinese grocery.

Chinese broccoli—A green stalked vegetable (*kai-lan* in Cantonese) that somehow acquired this name here in the States. It's sold as Chinese broccoli even in shops that cater mainly to Asian consumers.

Chinese chives—More garlicky than regular chives. However, you can substitute regular chives in a pinch.

Chinese pickled cabbage—This is sold in small cans at most Chinese markets. If you have any left over, store it in a plastic container.

Chinese sausage—Small, thin dry sausages with a texture similar to Mexican chorizo. Try to get them from a Chinese butcher if possible. Otherwise, the packaged ones will do.

Chipotle peppers—These are smoked chiles that are sold canned in a spicy sauce. You can get them in the Mexican section of most supermarkets.

Chorizo—Find this salami-like sausage in any Mexican or Latin American market.

Choy sum—Also referred to as choy sum cabbage. Similar to Chinese broccoli. Look for it in Asian grocery stores.

Coconut, shredded—Try to find the frozen product sold at Indian and Asian grocery shops. Otherwise, dried will do. Note that the recipes in the book always call for unsweetened coconut. Of course, if you live in a place with fresh coconuts, use fresh.

Coconut milk—Canned coconut milk is easy to find, but frozen—which you can buy in some Asian shops—tastes far better.

Curry leaves—Nothing at all to do with curries, curry powder, or curry paste. Instead, they're intensely flavorful leaves found in the produce section of Indian grocery stores. Look for dried curry leaves if you can't find fresh.

Curry paste—These days, you can find it in the Indian section of many supermarkets or on the shelves of Indian grocery stores. If you can't find it, use an equal amount of curry powder + a teaspoon of peanut oil instead.

Daikon—Large white radish that looks more like a huge, fat carrot. Surprisingly common once you know what to look for.

Dashi broth—A classic Japanese item. Find it as either a powder or liquid. Use the liquid if you can.

Deep-fried onions—Sold in large plastic bags or cans in Indian grocery stores. Use them sparingly; they're high in calories and impossible to stop eating from the bag once you start.

Dried shrimp—A staple in many Asian cuisines, these are easily found in Chinese supermarkets. Even though they're dried and relatively stable, I prefer to store them in a tightly sealed package in the fridge.

Dried shrimp paste—A paste made from dried shrimp. It's sold in small jars and found in Asian supermarkets.

Dry unseasoned breadcrumbs—You can find these in the supermarket. Read labels carefully to make sure there's no added salt or seasoning.

Durum semolina flour—Supermarkets with good baking sections will have it. Make sure it's both durum and semolina (see page 15).

Fish sauce—A salty liquid condiment used all over Southeast Asia. It's the color of a good lager beer and has a unique taste and fragrance you'll either love or hate.

Galangal root—Substitute frozen galangal—which many Asian grocery stores carry—when you can't find fresh.

Garam masala powder—Easily found in Indian grocery stores, and often stocked in the international section of supermarkets. Don't use whole garam masala instead!

Ginger garlic paste—Sold in glass jars. Easily found in Indian grocery stores.

Guanciale—Italian cured pork cheek. Substitute pancetta or even bacon if you can't find it.

Harissa—North African chile paste. Try to buy it in a reclosable glass jar instead of (the more easily found) cans.

Honeycomb tripe—Found at good butcher shops and Latin and Asian markets. Fresh tripe does not have a strong smell. If you detect more than a nice beefy fragrance, don't buy or use it.

Indian ice cream (*kulfi*)—Indian ice cream and *kulfi* are not exactly the same thing, but for our purposes, they're interchangeable. Real *kulfi* isn't aerated the same way as ice cream, so it's a bit denser. What counts, for me, though, are those amazing South Asian flavors like cardamom, rose, and saffron. Mango or pistachio ice cream from your regular source can be substituted.

Japanese fish cake (*kamaboko*)—Sold fresh in good Japanese markets, and frozen in Asian megamarts.

Korean chile pepper paste (*gochujang*)—Sold in plastic tubs at specialty Korean stores. It's very hot and can burn if it gets in your eyes or nostrils. Handle it with care!

Korean red pepper powder—A very hot and finely ground pepper. Substitute any really hot pepper powder if you can't find it.

Korean roasted black bean paste (*chunjang*)—Despite its name and color, *chunjang* is a thick paste made from fermented soybeans. It's easily found at Korean markets.

Laksa leaves—This ingredient goes by so many names, I don't know where to start. It is sold as Vietnamese mint, hot mint, *phak phai*, or *daun kesom*. Where I live, it's most commonly carried in Vietnamese markets, but can show up anyplace Southeast Asian ingredients are sold.

Lard—Try to get freshly rendered lard if you can. Good butcher shops sometimes have it. If you can't find it, use vegetable shortening instead. Those blocks of lard sold in cardboard boxes should be used only as a last resort.

Lemongrass—Lemongrass stalks look like fat hay and smell a bit like lemon. They're sold in Asian markets in bundles. There should be at least some green in them; avoid ones that are too brown and dried out.

Mirin—Japanese cooking sake. Look for it anyplace that sushi-making supplies are sold. In many parts of the country, you can find it in the local supermarket.

Miso paste—A thick paste made from fermented soybeans. Recipes in this book were tested with light miso, but any will work. Be aware that miso paste lasts forever; if you bought some a long time ago and have it lingering at the back of your fridge, use it.

Napa cabbage *kimchi*—This classic Korean preserved vegetable is always available in Korean shops and is finding its way into local supermarkets. Look for jars in the produce department.

Noodles—Ethnic grocery stores specializing in the cuisine of the recipe will have more variety than local supermarkets, and often lower prices too. These stores will sometimes have fresh forms of noodles—especially rice noodles—that are otherwise only found dried. Another advantage to ethnic markets is that you can often find advice on which brands local customers prefer.

Nori—Japanese seaweed sheets. These are the same thing that sushi rolls are wrapped in. They're sold flat-packed in supermarkets.

Oyster sauce—Sold in ketchup-like bottles in most Chinese departments and stores. Sometimes you can spot it in supermarket Asian departments.

Palm sugar—Palm sugar is similar to maple sugar but made from palm sap. It's sold in kiss-shaped blobs that are then packed in plastic containers. Buy it at grocery stores that sell Southeast Asian ingredients. When you're ready to use it, put the blobs in a plastic bag and smash them with a meat mallet.

Pancetta—Italian cured bacon. You can sometimes find it chopped and packaged in plastic containers at supermarket deli counters; otherwise, have it sliced for you and cut up the slices.

Pasta—Pretty much every shape called for in this book can be found in a good supermarket. For some reason, most brands I've used have instructions that call for overcooking—this has to be accepted as one of those mysteries of modern life.

Rice wine—Interchangeable with mirin and available at Chinese grocery shops (see listing above).

Rose syrup—Not rose water, but a syrup that resembles those used in fancy coffee shops. Find it in Indian grocery stores.

Saffron threads—Read the label! Many stores sell Chinese-grown saffron that's really cheap and completely tasteless. The reputable brands sold in supermarkets are brilliantly expensive but a reliable choice.

Sambal—The Maylasian chile paste is found in most Asian markets. Look for it in small glass jars.

Shallots—Shallots look like small red onions. They are sweeter and lend an authentic flavor to the dishes they're used in. Supermarkets often sell them in mesh bags.

Shiitake mushrooms, dried—The classic dried Chinese mushroom. They're a basic item at Chinese markets.

Shiitake mushrooms, fresh—These days, fresh shiitake mushrooms are sold all over the place, but they are much cheaper in Chinese markets.

Sichuan peppercorns—A Chinese spice that has its own unique zing; sort of like chile flakes with an added numbing power. Find it in Chinese markets.

Sichuan pickled mustard greens—Chinese grocery stores will carry these in both glass jars and clay crocks. Either will be fine.

Soy sauce, thick—Chinese grocery stores will sell it in wide-mouth jars. Don't substitute regular soy sauce; thick soy sauce is more similar to Korean roasted black bean paste (see listing above).

Tamarind concentrate—Look for the syrup in a glass jar, not the block of paste. Most Indian grocers carry it.

Thai chile garlic paste—Asian stores usually have it. Otherwise, go for similar products from Malaysia or Indonesia.

Thai pickled garlic cloves—Sold in jars at Thai markets.

Tofu, deep-fried and pressed—Both varieties are available at Chinese and other Asian grocery stores.

Tomatoes, canned crushed (called *passata* in Italian)—Much has been written elsewhere about San Marzano versus other varieties of canned tomatoes, but this isn't anywhere as important as freshness or crushing process. When you're in the store, examine the dates stamped on the cans and the list of ingredients. There should be no added water, seasonings or preservatives. Read carefully and buy accordingly. Price is no indicator of quality here!

Tukmaria seeds—Often called *falooda* seeds, they are actually the seeds of the holy basil plant. Find them in Indian grocery shops.

Urad dhal—A type of lentil found at Indian grocery stores.

Wakame (seaweed)—A classic ingredient in both Japanese and Korean cuisines, *wakame* can be found at grocery stores specializing in these countries. You can also find it—at a much higher price, of course—at health food stores.

INDEX